SHANSHUI CITY

MA YANSONG

If the ancient city concerned religion,

And the modern city concerns capital and power,

Then the city of the future should concern

people and nature.

The Architecture of Ma Yansong

Kenya HARA

Humanity has designed a rectilinear world. We have divided the earth into rectangular plots, covered them with a rectangular grid of roads, and then lined the roads with rectangular buildings. We walk through rectangular entrances, ride rectangular elevators, turn at right-angled corners through rectangular hallways, and then open rectangular doors to find rectangular rooms waiting inside. The rectangular rooms are outfitted with pieces of furniture, matched with rectangular windows. We look out these windows and see the rectangular silhouette of the city. The table, furniture, television, and remote control are also rectangular. Lest we forget, we tap away at rectangular computer keyboards on rectangular desks. We write on rectangular sheets of stationary which will finally be folded into rectangular envelopes to which rectangular postage stamps are affixed. The postmark on top of the stamp, though, is occasionally round.

At the same time we also find that manhole covers are round. This is by necessity. If they were square they might fall through the manhole. Planets, including the earth, are also round. The reasons for this may seem obvious now, though we must remember that humanity required the aid of science to discover the sphere. Reviewing the history of science, we can see that knowledge of the earth's roundness developed in tandem with a number of other advances concerning the sphere. One could say that when humankind began experimenting with spheres, the mysteries of the universe were opened to us.

Shapes are the inevitable products of humankind's interaction with the environment. As if echoing the bilateral symmetry of the human body, the rectilinear sheet of paper was born. The precision of the sphere reminds us of the principles of the universe, and that superior design responds to the universality of human behavior. Thus we see square tables, the four prongs of a fork, and round manholes.

However, Ma Yansong does not design rectilinear buildings. What he aims to capture are organic forms reminiscent of natural stone. His work directly confronts the relationship between the body and form and attempts to rationally integrate them, presenting an exterior design that appears as emanating ripples. Through this, he has established his unique position within the industry.

The logic of production, planning, collection, and distribution has nurtured the growth of the rectangle. However, this may be nothing more than a reflection of the superficiality and emptiness of human knowledge. Ask yourself: Why do humans design their environment into rectangles? Observation reveals that rectangles do not exist within the natural world. One must admit a certain number of rectlinear phenomena, but these are essentially unstable, and thus it is very difficult to find a specific embodiment of the shape. By comparison, triangles are more stable than rectangles.

Yet human beings have encouraged the development of this rare form to the point of its current dominance. The leading lights of Western-born Modernism, including Le Corbusier, Mies van der Rohe, and others, were all advocates of the square. In the seminal works of Dutch Plasticism, which took radicalism for its canon, right angles are ubiquitous. However, if we attempt to approach the wisdom of nature, or the truths of the universe, we are confronted with a natural world devoid of rectangles. Will we not pick up a single pebble from this expanse of nature and investigate the structure of its form?

Ancient China sought wisdom within the natural phenomena of surging waves, towering mountains, and formless wind. China stood at the forefront, pushing the bounds of human knowledge. Today, Ma seeks to capture this wisdom and inspiration within architectural form, a program I believe to be perfectly in tune with the needs of our times. I have named this wisdom-as-form "Shanshui."

This book is structured around photographs of Ma's architectural models. From realized architectural works we can clearly understand the architect's style; however, if we wish to understand Ma's sensibilities more profoundly, we must examine his models. This is because the limited architectural technology of today cannot completely express the full range of Ma's perception, whereas models can more clearly depict the direction of his explorations. As such, they appear more sensuous and true than his completed architectural works. To Ma, books are like stones: they are representatives of primitive feeling and, unmediated perception. This point is essential when discussing his philosophy of design.

As a medium for "Shanshui," an architectural mode of thought informed by Eastern philosophy, this book is a milestone worthy of commemoration. Its influence will be immeasurable.

Kenya HARA | Designer

Kenya Hara (b. 1958) emphasizes the design of both objects and experiences. He is considered a leading design personality in Japan. He has been the art director of Muji since 2001 and designed the opening and closing ceremony programs of the Nagano Winter Olympic Games 1998. Several books written by Hara, including *Designing Design* and *White*, have been translated into a number of languages, including other Asian languages.

SHANSHUI CITY

MA YANSONG

Preface

Hans Ulrich Obrist and Lorenza Baroncelli

In many ways the history of architecture is the re-assembly of fragments of utopian projects based on the naive and irrepressible desire to make the world a better place. What architects frequently forget is that these countless material gestures unfold within the chaotic, uncontrollable, and "untheorized" landscape of everyday life. The practice of intertwining universal doctrines with local existing conditions is as epic and unpredictable as any medieval crusade.

The history of twentieth century cities in Asia has been influenced by the desire for a perfect "modernity." While North American cities that grew out of the Modernist period have begun a process of decline, Chinese cities have challenged one another to create a faster, higher, more superlative "American Chinese Dream." New and old cities have been rocked by the shockwave of new and highly concentrated wealth, struggling to compensate for the imbalance between modernization and tradition through shifts between openness, freedom, criticism, oppression, and resistance.

This process of confrontation and exchange has generated some very innovative, but also controversial models of architectural/urban concepts and practice, which are specific to each particular context. According to Rem Koolhaas, Chinese urban growth has brought about a kind of "City of Exacerbated Difference (COED)," which "is not the methodical creation of the ideal, but the opportunistic exploitation of flukes, accidents, and imperfections." Implying a process of cultural translation, Asia's urban explosion has also afforded access to other cultures.

The new urban model generated by the Asian economic explosion of the 1980s and 1990s is nowadays exported to other continents. For example, it is enough to take a virtual bird's-eye tour on Google Earth to catch China's visible impact on urban development in Africa. China's economic and political growth has made it a significant player on the continent. Not only Africa's single largest trading partner today, China's practical investment in hands-on diplomacy—offering buildings, roads, railways, power plants, and other infrastructure—has emerged as a powerful alternative to Western development aid which, in contrast, is geared towards reducing poverty. This has led to Chinese companies successfully funding and building many new developments in African cities, ranging from the headquarters of the African Union in Addis Ababa, Ethiopia, to the Lekki Free Trade Zone in Lagos, Nigeria.

If we were to merely follow the course of history as a linear process, we would not be surprised to discover cities engaged in a twenty-first century "Chinese Dream" of a fast and technological economic explosion. However, architects such as Ma Yansong are there to remind us that there are alternative ways of approaching urbanism.

Criticizing an extremely rationalist ideology and simplified reading of Western modernism, Ma proposes different models of urban development which are based on a re-balance between post-global modernity and local necessity, between linear growth and "irrational" intuition, between progress and tradition, in order to create both human and urban spaces. These gestures are often temporal interruptions of high-speed urban transformation that open a kind of "emptiness," or moments of suspense in the very core of an urban plan: détournements, supplements, shifts, or disturbances amid traffic and business.

For Ma the process is more important than the final object.

In Hutong Bubble, for example, the project created for Beijing 2050, he surgically inserts bubbles of modernity into the courtyards around Beijing's Forbidden City. Instead of fragmenting old buildings in order to renovate them, Ma provides new functions for people and activates life within them. Following Cedric Price's ideas,

Ma's cities do not require entirely new neighborhoods, but only envisage "magnets" inserted into old neighborhoods to re-stimulate them. One contains a bathroom, another a staircase, a studio, or playground; Hutong Bubble shares dreams like confetti across the old city.

Hutong Bubble realizes the future before it arrives.

As the Metabolists focused Modernist spaces away from Euro-centrism to the "symbiosis of diverse cultures, from anthropocentrism to ecology, from industrial to information society, from universalism to the age of symbiosis of diverse elements, from the age of the machine to the age of the life principle." (Kisho Kurokawa), Ma once again highlights ecological issues as being central to the future of urban development.

Currently, the rapid decline of the Asian environment is noteworthy, as ironically, the pursuit of a harmonious relationship between humankind and nature has always been an integral part of the East Asian tradition. This is seen as presenting a liberating alternative to the dominant Western model of urbanization and, significantly, as the voice of the "other" in the current process of globalization. The re-introduction of a central role of nature in architecture, of a more contextual, pragmatic approach is a cultural strategy to confront and resist the domination of Western modernism and post-modernism in the processes of globalization.

Urban Forest, the high-rise tower for the most recent urban center of China, Chongqing, differs from a standard skyscraper and presents itself as an urban landmark that expresses a devotion to nature. With its dizzying silhouette, it is simultaneously "alive" and imperfect. This imperfection allows people to live in harmony with this human-made structure.

Furthermore, Fake Hills, the residential apartment block in Beihai Park, is obviously not a real mountain or parametric landscape, but reproduces the image of a natural scene. It transcends pure form and emphasizes an artistic mood.

Ma's efforts to create an original model of modernization, to rather be in-between geographies than to belong to a fixed geography, can be seen as a contribution to the enrichment of the current global urban development.

This publication is a chronicle of Ma's explorations of an "intensified" landscape. It is about projects, but also about daily practice for, and in, the city. Combining the principles of nature and geomantic technologies, West and East, past and future, buildings and emotions, this book intends to present an innovative vision of a post-global city, which is at once harmonious with nature and also connected to the global cyber-network.

It is a manifesto for a new global vernacular for the age of technological supremacy of the landscape.

We are looking forward to see Ma's Lucas Museum of Narrative Art in Chicago, the first cultural project designed by a Chinese architect in the West. As Douglas Gordon stated, "It has only just begun."

Hans Ulrich Obrist | Art Curator, Critic and Historian of Art

Obrist is Co-director of Exhibitions and Programmes and Director of International Projects at the Serpentine Gallery, London. His travels and curatorial work over past 20 years transcend borders, granting him a profound understanding of global contemporary art and significant influence over its ongoing development.

Lorenza Baroncelli | Architect, Researcher and Independent Curator

Baroncelli is scientific director of the Swiss pavilion curated by Hans Ulrich Obrist at the Venice Architecture Biennale 2014 and co-founder of the *Tomorrow*, the first daily journal about the future of Europe.

SHANSHUI CITY

Origins

To most people in China, Shanshui is a traditional style of painting, translated literally as "mountains and water." They believe these ink landscape paintings represent a pre-modern understanding of the natural world. I, however, do not see it this way. I believe there are some things that arise from antiquity, yet remain connected to our future.

The East Asian perception of the world is imbued with a special affinity for nature: "I am part of you, and you are part of me." Since the Industrial Revolution, history has been marked by over a century of humankind subjugating and transforming nature. Towering concrete skyscrapers serve as monuments to power and capital in contempt of human nature. People simultaneously love and despise the city, vacillating between the impulse to remain or to flee. Today, the North American cities that sprang up during the Modernist period are in decline, while Chinese cities are growing at breakneck speed, competing to build a faster, taller, more powerful American-style "Chinese Dream".

China must consider the long-term future: fifty to a hundred years hence. When this phase of urbanization has ended, what will we have contributed to humankind's urban culture? A new kind of thinking must be developed, one that does not rely on imitation of the West, simple pragmatism, or the idealization of the past.

The future development of society demands that we reconsider the relationship between humanity and nature. We must carefully reevaluate our experience of an industrial civilization that forfeited our natural environment. We have to find a new path, one that restores a sense of harmony and balance to our relationship with the natural world.

Shanshui is an idealized worldview developed by the ancient Chinese through extended contact with the natural world, a worldview that integrates the everyday life of humanity with the impulse to seek spiritual refuge in nature. In the face of China's rapid urbanization, however, the mountain retreats and private gardens depicted in Shanshui paintings have become dreams only attainable by the most privileged. The time is ripe for architects to delineate a new ideal for the city of the future, to gradually construct an urban environment that embodies both the convenience of the modern city and the ancient Eastern affinity for the natural world. Such a city would combine urban density and functionality with the aesthetic and philosophical ideals of Shanshui. It would be a city of the future built upon a foundation of spiritual and cultural values, a city to be shared and enjoyed by all residents, one that we might call a "Shanshui City."

This Shanshui City is not simply an eco-city, or a garden-city, nor does it imply modeling the city's architecture on natural forms such as mountains. Rather, it represents humanity's affinity for the natural world, and our quest for inner fulfillment, as expressed in philosophies of the East. The challenge will be whether these philosophical musings can be manifested through large-scale urban planning. It may be that the current crisis of the city will herald the arrival of a new order of urban civilization.

Chapter 1

The Soulless Modern City

Stock Cities

I'm a little scared,
the sky is getting gloomy.
Chi Peng, photograph (detail), 2008.

I have been to many cities and to me they are like supermarkets. The shelves are full of eye-catching objects, but the contents don't differ much from one store to the next. Works of architecture, whether mundane or extravagant, are exhibited like products on shelves, arranged by function, waiting to be bought. Perhaps one store's products differ slightly from another's, but the overall sense of sameness is overwhelming. Cities have begun to feel like copies of one another. My impressions of them are muddled to the point that I can't even be sure which ones I've visited before. This even holds true for cities I've explored multiple times and ought to know quite well. I've been considering this question for a long time: Why do the cities being built today all look so alike?

The stocking shelves used in supermarkets are designed for very specific purposes. They can easily be replicated, mass produced, and stocked with goods—scalability of production and sales are the main considerations. Modernist cities are built along similar lines, as if they were giant stocking shelves. Land development costs and efficiency of use guide city planning, resulting in the construction of block grids. Land prices are meted out according to location within the city and developers have to bid against one another. Architecture has become the product that occupies land, providing maximum usable floor space and stylish exterior packaging. Cities are becoming increasingly utilitarian and commoditized, and it has become difficult to consider the emotional needs of residents when a city's development is solely governed by benefit modeling. During this wave of rapid urbanization, "stock cities" have become the most effective model for growth. Propelled by a constant influx of capital and surplus consumption, these urban "stock shelves" are congested and lack character. The requirements of capital and the need for rapid development forces many central business districts, technology parks, industrial parks, and residential developments to be built according to the stock model. A stock city, however, does not provide emotional refuge for its residents and pays no heed to the feeling and experience of living within it. This model of the city has reached its limits.

What would a city outside of this stock shelf model look like? During the early stages of urbanization in Japan, the Metabolism School emerged. This school was comprised of the architects Otaka Masato,

Zhen Fumihiko, Kisho Kurokawa, Kiyonori Kikutake, and the critic, Noboru Kawazoe, all of whom were influenced by Kenzo Tange. They believed that urban and architectural growth were similar to an organism's metabolism—i.e. dynamic. They emphasized the growth, transformation, and decay of objects. During the late 1950s and early 1960s, these Japanese architects and critics gradually formed their own architectural philosophy. They developed an independent contemporary architectural system based on their aesthetic and ideological principles, becoming the first non-Western avant-garde school of architectural thought. Although they sought a path to the future through the spirit of traditional Japanese culture, on the whole they were strong proponents of using industrial technology to resolve practical dilemmas. The reason the Metabolism Movement ultimately lost momentum is that it did not foresee the arrival of the information revolution thirty years later; instead, it remained focused on industrial technology in large-scale urban construction. However, operating as a common architectural vision, the Metabolism Movement gave one cohort of architects the power to transcend the restrictions of their time. I admire the tremendous mental effort and energy they dedicated to this program.

In the end, however, a city is more than just an organism, just as a human being is not merely bones, and flesh, and physiological functions. Like each human, each city has its own spirit. Technology can only solve certain material problems; it cannot resolve issues affecting the spirit of a city, nor can it resolve humanity's crisis of feeling. Our modern cities lack an inner spirituality; or rather, they lack a soul.

What, then, is the soul of a city?

Chicks on the Production Line

The photo to the right depicts the final moment in the life of the chicks. Within moments it will cease to exist, sharing the same fate as some two million other male chicks. These creatures live for a brief moment before the conveyer belt tosses them into the shredder. Feed can not be wasted on a male chick that will never produce eggs. They are living organisms reduced to waste products. In some ways we are not very different from these chicks, trapped, as we are in a modern urban society that reveres efficiency and pragmatism. The stock city is purely

Chicks about to be destroyed on the production line.

functional, a city with no soul. It is a highly efficient factory, constantly devouring resources and pumping out waste. To be more precise, it is like a meatpacking plant, and as long as we stay on the conveyor belt, we need not worry about survival or food... at least for a short time. Since the Industrial Revolution, cities have expanded at an almost unimaginable pace. Hundreds of millions of migrants have flooded into cities from the countryside. The immense productive capacity unleashed by mechanization compels the unthinking construction of factories in urban areas. Life in large cities is controlled by the rhythm of industrial production. To keep machines in continuous operation, production workers are given shifts that span all hours of the day and night. In the film *Modern Times*, Charlie Chaplin plays a worker who frantically turns screws on an assembly line and is force-fed by machine. Ultimately, it is only by losing his senses that he finally finds freedom.

Although today's urban centers are occupied by office buildings and commercial strips, the basic features of this "meatpacking society" have not undergone any fundamental change. In both the industrial and the post-industrial era, the mechanisms of competition, assembly-line production, profit maximization, and recreational consumption are the main drivers of the central economic model. These are the forces behind the constant expansion of cities. Everything is a procedure within a vast production plant. Humans and animals alike become products and/or components on the production line. We are like pieces of meat waiting to be injected with hormones and antibiotics, and processed for consumption. Unlike the chicks in the photo, we will survive the process of commoditization, only to be consumed by society according to our usefulness once we are "placed on the shelf." Education is merely one production line within this massive factory. It instills us with a system of social values at the expense of freedom and individuality, preparing us for what appears to be a secure existence with this society-cum-slaughterhouse.

I cannot help but ask, haven't we sacrificed enough to this modern "meatpacking civilization," which operates in direct opposition to our nature?

Monuments to Capital and Power

After the rapid urban development of the Industrial Revolution, the favored position that cities once granted to the sacred became occupied by capital and power. With the efficiency of modern mass production, cities became increasingly similar to one another. Standardized architecture was developed that could be put into use in any locale, for any project. Forced to survive in a world of continuous architectural replication, people lost their emotional connection to their environment. They increasingly became mere implements indoctrinated with the values of the competitive marketplace. The slogan of the eighth Olympic games in 1924, "Faster, Higher, Stronger" seemed to herald a new era in which competition would be the means of survival. Our lives are affected by many different types of competition. This viewpoint dominates the psychological orientation of modern society. Competition between cities is often expressed through architectural monuments that symbolize wealth and power. It was this urban competition that gave rise to the skyscraper.

The Shard, London, UK,
Renzo Piano, 2012.

Ryugyong Hotel, Pyongyang,
North Korea, 1988–2012.

Modern urban buildings expand skyward, reaching ever-greater heights. This impulse seems to originate from the human instinct for competition. From Egyptian pyramids and obelisks, to Greek temples and Gothic cathedrals; all were attempts to occupy the visual higher ground and convey power. People are in awe of objects that tower above them. These edifices have the authority to impose insignificance, to define the center, to gather the masses. Height exerts direct control over the psyche. Before industrial civilization, religion occupied a central role in people's lives. Religious buildings would naturally be larger than residences to express the central role of the divine and the respect for religious leaders and institutions. In the industrial era, machines toppled the divine from its altar. Religious architecture retreated from the stage of history, to be replaced by even taller commercial skyscrapers, symbols of power and capital. This ambition to reach new heights has resulted in thoughtless urban sprawl and the competitive flaunting of wealth and power.

The Shard, designed by architect Renzo Piano, was recently completed in London. Like a sword piercing the sky, this 310-meter tower is Europe's tallest building. Ironically, it reminds me of the Ryugyong Hotel in Pyongyang. Both are vertical spires that rise into the clouds, reminiscent of Gothic cathedrals. The difference is that while Gothic spires symbolize closeness to God, these two modern spires each have a more profane significance: one embodies the financial ambitions of Britain, while the other is an icon of one of the last bastions of communism. One deifies wealth, the other deifies power. One is a monument to capitalism, the other to communism, yet, ironically, they possess nearly identical visual forms.

This competitive trend has spread globally, giving form to the ambitions of every nation. These buildings are the physical embodiment of capital and power. They project the confidence of the state, yet these traits are unrelated to the imagination and spiritual needs of a city's residents. Political systems and investment groups have replaced the divine, inheriting its control over the world. Cities have been reduced to material shells, and have ceased to be refuges for the soul. People, once again, are deemed to be insignificant.

The American architect, Robert Venturi advocated taking lessons from Las Vegas. Without tourism, Las Vegas would probably be a ghost town. Its form of prosperity only appeals to lost souls. This city-cum-casino is a site for pure consumption. Like failed rust-belt cities, Las Vegas is a site for accumulating the wreckage of thwarted dreams and desires. Detroit in its heyday represented the prosperity and ambitions of the American automobile industry, but eventually fell prey to its own utilitarian ambition and misplaced values. And Detroit is by no means the only city to have declined into a spiral of rising unemployment, soaring crime rates, and fleeing populations. These cities are the products of a certain period of industrialization. As soon as the structure of industry shifts and profits migrate, these cities fall into rapid decline. One suspects it is only a matter of time before Las Vegas begins to manifest the symptoms of its spiritual illness.

Cities are the birthplace of civilization and the meeting place of humanity; we both love and hate them at the same time. The afflictions of the modern city are nearly universal. Many old cities are losing their souls, while new cities can't seem to find them in the first place. This condition appears to be the norm for our era.

A House Is Not a Machine for Living In

Le Corbusier is undoubtedly the leading figure of Modernist architecture, and a symbol of architecture's revolutionary spirit. He translated the impact of the latest advances of industrialization into architectural terms, and embraced the new era with unrivalled passion. His premise was that a new epoch required new buildings: "We must start over completely from zero." In his book, *Towards a New Architecture* published in 1923, Le Corbusier provocatively wrote: "A house is a machine for living in." This statement was affirmed by architectural practice during the post-war energy crisis and housing shortage. When housing issues become so critical they impact political and social stability, thinking about buildings is no longer just an architectural concern. Rather, architecture is recognized as being a political method for resolving social problems. Houses became "machines for living in" out of historical necessity. Times have since changed, but the modern city is still full of "machines for living in." When the drive for commercial profits replaces the requirements of living, that is to say, when houses are reduced to mere mass-produced products, they will become estranged from the basic essence of a home. This further intensifies the mechanization of residential functions. We need to realize that no specific people are implied in the sentence "houses are machines for living in." The statement assumes that residents are abstract, standardized units. It simplifies and quantifies their needs to reach a convergent ideal; it is driven by the requirements of industrial production, rather than people's emotional or spiritual needs.

The Marseille apartment building, designed in Le Corbusier's later period, has had a profound impression on me as an architect. Le Corbusier's thinking at the time was set against the backdrop of his idealism concerning the future. The Marseille apartment is highly innovative; there are mid-level public spaces, elevated walkways, split levels, rooftop gardens.... It is social housing that emphasizes the dignity of living. Yet so many years later, why has there been no revolutionary progress in this direction? Do residents of the modern city live with the kind of dignity that Corbusier envisioned? Buildings today are largely still four-sided boxes, built with great efficiency and advanced technology, but for the most part they are not nearly as evocative as Le Corbusier's Marseille apartment building.

Cities today offer great luxury for the wealthy and unbearable overcrowding for the underprivileged. Land is becoming increasingly scarce, so building upward is the only option for many large cities. Today's cities generally operate on old theories, driven by the instinct for survival. How much longer can the machines for living of the big city continue to lumber along before we lose our minds? Will the modern buildings already inundating our cities continue to reproduce at the same breakneck pace, or will we intervene to replace them with something more humane? To do so, we must develop a methodolgy to address our current living situation. Given that so many urban citizens already live in high-rise buildings, how do we create more humane spaces that will bring people together, promote face-to-face interaction, and deepen social structures?

Machines are both products of industrial production and the means of production, but machines can't produce emotion or thought. What they satisfy are merely the mass production requirements of society. However, housing should first and foremost address people as their subject, and the human need for emotional belonging as their primary consideration. The difficulty with big cities does not lie in skyscrapers or high-rises per se, rather it is the values concealed within those buildings which lead to the loss of our humanity and our sense of spiritual emptiness. Cities should be wellsprings of humanistic spirit and free will, but today we feel encumbered by the material shackles and desperate urgency of city life. We live in a time of technological advancement and material abundance, yet we are deficient in thought and emotionally numb. Urban housing should not be reduced to machines for living in!

China is developing at a historically unprecedented speed, and cities of all tiers are engaged in construction of near-incalculable scale; this urbanization process is replicating the living-machine-model on a massive scale, crowding out traditional housing and modes of living. This kind of urban development model, copied from the West, is creating a rift between history and reality. We have lost our roots, and our cities have lost the philosophical spirit and humanity they once embodied. Though as young architects we spend long hours hunched over our work, immersed in contemporary architectural trends, we must also lift our heads above the fray and consider the road ahead. We must chart a path to the future.

Masterpieces of Anti-Modernism

Domino System, Le Corbusier, 1914.

Le Corbusier proposed breaking away from classicism, molding architecture to the criteria of industrial society. His famed Five Points of Architecture established a standard for this:

1. Free-standing pilotis
2. Free floor plans
3. Free façades
4. Long, horizontal ribbon windows
5. Roof gardens

These five elements are like a machine in their simplicity and effectiveness, and are a powerful rejection of classicism. With *The Radiant City* (1935), Le Corbusier enthusiastically proposed the use of the five elements in a residential unit to realize a compact, high-efficiency model for a new city. He imagined using spacious, mass-produced residences to realize social equality, high-speed transportation such as cars to erase the distinction between cities and suburbs, and elevated roads to return the ground plane to pedestrians. This kind of homogenous modern city would provide sunlight, green trees, and open space as the foundations for basic happiness, and realize the individual freedom of the machine age. But reality does not always follow our intentions. When mechanically applied to numerous urban construction projects, Le Corbusier's socially transformative vision resulted in the proliferation of crude residential buildings, an incursion of automobiles, and a sprawling, ever expanding network of roads.

Late in his professional life, Le Corbusier produced the chapel of Notre Dame du Haut, which deviated sharply from his five elements. I believe the chapel is the work in which Le Corbusier traveled the greatest spiritual distance. It is a building that pursues the eternal, responding to a call that has manifested in every period of human history. By way of contrast, the five elements of Modernist architecture only operate within the framework of the industrial era, and are concerned exclusively with form, function, and standards. They are abstractions that turn away from humanity and are bereft of the human spirit. Ironically, the greatest architectural works of the Modernist period did not make use of the Five Points, while the vast number of buildings that followed these tenets have clogged our cities with their vacuous forms.

The chapel of Notre Dame du Haut in Ronchamp, France, Le Corbusier, 1950–1953.

The chapel of Notre Dame du Haut in Ronchamp is abstract and sculptural. It disregards the call to soaring heights. Critics have commented a great deal on its exterior; some say the roof looks like a large ship, linking it to the mechanical aesthetics advocated by Le Corbusier; others say it resembles a bishop's hat or two hands held in prayer. Regardless of what its form might evoke, this building cannot be explained through Modernist theory. The chapel eschews narrow steeple towers and features freely placed stained-glass windows. The building manages to escape from the confines of Modernism: the frontal façade is absent, the entire building stands unified in the midst of nature, defying expectations for religious architecture with its almost anthropomorphic appearance. Yet its interior retains an intensely spiritual ambiance. The irregular openings allow unexpected rays of colored light to penetrate the dimly lit space, creating a sacred atmosphere similar to traditional churches. Sunlight enters from the side, rather than from above, suggesting that the divine surrounds us, urging us to inward reflection.

Chapel on the Water, Japan, Tadao Ando, 1988.

Compared with the chapel of Notre Dame du Haut, Japanese architect, Tadao Ando's Chapel on the Water and the Church of the Light represent a further step along these lines of development. Although these two buildings are still Modernist in form, they nevertheless represent a betrayal of the doctrines of Modernism. The Church of the Light is located on a street corner on the outskirts of Osaka. The floor area is only slightly larger than one hundred square meters; its entrance is inconspicuous. It is a small church capable of holding only one hundred worshippers, barely larger than a single-story home, but through it Ando transmits an extraordinary spiritual power. At the end of a narrow sloping path a cross-shaped opening is visible on a level with the worshippers. Sunlight gently penetrates through the opening, without any sense of distance, as though heaven could simply be found on the other side of the wall.

Ando's Chapel on the Water is completely open to the natural world. Within it worshippers feel that they are a part of nature itself. However, Ando's nature is not the nature of primeval ecology, rather it is a nature possessed of consciousness which shares an affinity with the human spirit, an abstraction of pure ecology mediated by the human mind. The pool facing the Chapel on the Water is supplied from a nearby stream. The depth of the pool was meticulously calculated to allow surface ripples to subtly convey the presence of the wind. These two churches both produce a meditative atmosphere. They use no tricks to inspire awe, no piercing rays of light, no towering heights. In these breathtaking spaces visitors can attune themselves to the changes of the four seasons, the eternal march of time, and the cycles of life. Ando's sacred spaces embody the direct realization of Zen, and a distinctly Eastern philosophical outlook on nature and life.

Fallingwater, USA,
Frank Lloyd Wright, 1936.

Fallingwater, designed by American architect Frank Lloyd Wright, was completed during the period of societal self-reflection and recovery that followed America's Great Depression. This residence, built above a waterfall, extends outwards from two boulders, its wide, horizontal hanging terraces and rough stone walls interlocking and interpenetrating. The water flows from directly beneath the building, creating an environment where building and nature merge into one. Natural scenery, the tactile experience of stone, and the sounds of wind and water permeate every corner of the structure. The building appears as though it grew naturally from the landscape of stone and water, sublimating nature and habitation into a greater whole. The staircase on the lowest level cantilevered terrace leads down to the stream's edge, creating a connection between residents, dwelling, and earth. The man who commissioned the building, Edgar Kaufman, donated Fallingwater to the American government after Wright passed away. In his speech Kaufman said Fallingwater is "a work of art, beyond any ordinary measure of excellence... House and site together form the very image of man's desire to be at one with nature, equal and wedded to nature... It is a public asset rather than a privately owned treasure." Though buildings incorporating more advanced technology can be found almost anywhere in the US, Fallingwater remains one of the masterpieces of American architectural history. It exists as an act of rebellion against Modernism in both principle and form, and serves as testament to the fact that a building is not granted a soul by virtue of the technology it employs.

Wright stands out among American-born architects due to the Asian cultural influences he absorbed during his sojourn in Japan. I have always wondered: Would a skyscraper designed by Wright have expressed the same spiritual fusion of nature and humanity found in Fallingwater? Later, I inadvertently came across a little-known sketch of a high-rise by Wright; it appeared similar to the post-modern residential buildings that congest China's cities today. I am intrigued by ambiguities within the thinking of this architect who had such deep reverence for the natural world. On one hand, he felt that the modern metropolis

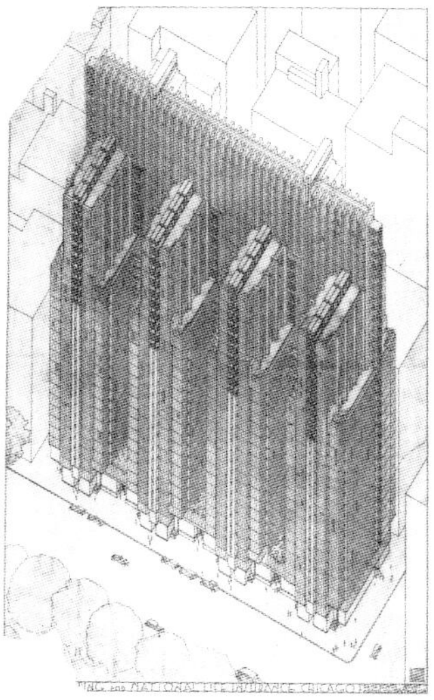

National Life Insurance Company Building, Chicago, Frank Lloyd Wright, 1924.

Salk Institute, USA, Louis Kahn, 1959–1965.

ought to be replaced with something on a scale that better represented human aspirations. On the other hand, he viewed the automobile as a driver of democracy. He felt widespread adoption of the automobile was necessary to aid the dispersion of dense urban populations. His ideals encouraged the "suburbanization" of America, but without the hoped-for elimination of the large city. His concept for Broadacre City failed to have a constructive impact on the modern city. Commuting by car between suburb and city has intensified the twin afflictions of traffic congestion and air pollution, not reduced them. Clearly, the problems of the big city are not resolved by denying the city's existence.

Looking back on China's urbanization over the past three decades, it is clear that architects, intellectuals, and thinkers have failed to make any significant contributions to the architectural pursuit of a new urban ideal. They have surrendered to the demands of pragmatism. I cannot help but wonder: Confronted with the twin forces of capital and power, has humanity already given up on the soul of the city?

The last modern building of enduring spirit that I wish to discuss is the Salk Institute designed by Louis Kahn. The first time I visited was in the dark of night and the entrance gate was locked; my visit began with me scaling the wall. Entering the complex I felt an inner trembling I had never experienced before. When I stood in the center of the courtyard, facing the inky black ocean and sky, I felt I was confronting an enormous black hole. The way ahead seemed unfathomable. This awe, bordering on terror, was completely unlike the tranquil and sublime atmosphere I later experienced during the daytime. To my mind, this building is sacred, producing an intense sense of place. Its layout mirrors the central symmetry and twin colonnades of an ancient Greek temple. Yet it differs in that the culmination of the central axis is free, opening to the ocean and sky, as if some deity were enshrined far beyond the horizon. One could say this building engages in a dialogue with nature. Or better yet, the poetic interaction of building and nature invites us to engage in a dialogue with ourselves. I believe that this sentiment will still be felt by visitors to this site a century from now. Architecture of this order connects with our natural affinities, creating an allure that transcends time.

Manhattan's Tomorrow

The Century with Mushroom Clouds, New York, Cai Guoqiang, 1996.

As the model modern city, New York has always held a particular fascination for me: it is complex, contradictory, and brimming with vitality. The great skyscrapers of every era are gathered here, but there are three landmarks in particular that seem most representative of the spirit of New York. They are the World Trade Center, the Empire State Building, and Central Park. Construction began on the Empire State Building in 1930, and was completed a year later, in 1931. Construction of a building of this height required the most advanced technology of the era as well as vast quantities of capital. In fact, at roughly the same time, the construction of the Palace of the Soviets in the Soviet Union was canceled due to lack of funds and adequate technology. However, I do not consider capital and technology to be the most important factors in the construction of these New York landmarks. More important was the idealism of the city planners of that era, particularly in the case of Central Park. Many cities have open, green spaces, but Central Park is unique in scale, ambition, intricacy of planning, and the significant role it plays in the city's life. To a great degree, Central Park has shaped the spirit of New York by imparting a sense of belonging to New Yorkers regardless of background or socio-economic means.

During the summer of 2001, I did an internship in New York at the architecture practice of Peter Eisenman. In August of that year I ascended the World Trade Center for the first time, and less than a month later, on September 11, the towers were destroyed. The atmosphere of New York was entirely changed by the catastrophe of that fateful day. The highly energetic, vital, and ambitious mood of the city was replaced by paralysis, shock, and sorrow. You could say that in a very short period of time, New York had revealed the full range of its emotions to me.

In 2002 we were given the topic "World Trade Center Rebuilt" for our graduation projects. At the time many of our professors were, in fact, participating in the World Trade Center Site Memorial Competition. The work of my fellow students displayed a wide range of perspectives. Some felt that a monument would be more appropriate, while others used the opportunity to envision the skyscraper of the future. As I set to work on my design, I realized I had never before dealt with such a complex and sensitive set of requirements. The training that I had received in analysis, concept, and development of idea did not seem applicable here. The first half of the semester was spent analyzing New

York's skyscrapers and the history of the city, nevertheless I was still unable to reach any specific conclusions. For a long time I was tortured by the sense that I was not making progress, despite all my efforts. Perhaps it was due to the sense of personal suffering I felt while working on this project, but one night I dreamed of a cloud that appeared over New York. This dream-vision became my inspiration. I would not design a monument commemorating the past, nor a skyscraper to set the standard for the future. Rather, I would create a floating city of the future, somewhat detached from reality, which would provide a kind of regenerative power.

Ground Zero, 9/11 Memorial Park, 2014.

The collapse of the twin towers signaled that the glorious reign of the Modernist skyscraper was nearing its end. While the political, ideological, and technical ramifications of the towers' collapse have generated much debate, the terrorist attacks of September 11th unquestionably remain one of the most concentrated focal points of sorrow in human history. Thus I hoped that my floating island would provide a kind of emotional relief to the people of New York. Climbing to the heights of the park, visitors would be rewarded with a vista of lakes and forests detached from history and time, perhaps allowing visitors to transcend temporal differences, be they political or ethnic.

I called my design the Floating Island because it both hovered above New York City and drew together the forest of concrete towers of Manhattan. The concept was to have a massive organic structure within the rectilinear city grid, supporting a suspended garden and lake. The people of the city would be liberated from the dim, bustling crevices between towering skyscrapers. They would be empowered to ascend into the sky where they could enjoy the warm sun, green space, and views of the New York skyline.

Floating Island calls into question the mechanical aesthetics and vertical cities of modernism. It celebrates human, emotional, and natural aesthetics. I feel that for New York, the best way to commemorate September 11 is to continue to grow and develop as a city. The design goal for the site ought to have been to open up a new chapter in the development of urban culture. Yet what transpired demonstrated to me that New York was no longer the vigorous and energetic city it had been; it seemed to have lost some of its courage and creativity.

Floating Island: Rebuilt WTC, New York, Ma Yansong, 2001.

Manhattan boasts a collection of the greatest skyscrapers of every age. When discussing the city of the future, it seems one should start with New York. I have long hoped that in New York I would be able to find someone crazy enough to help me to realize my vision for the city of the future; thus I had a meeting with a real estate developer who was open to listening to some of my ideas.

Our meeting was held on the highest floor of World Trade Center, Building Seven. For the first time I had an aerial view of ground zero from forty floors above. The September 11 memorial is surrounded by several high-rise office buildings. In the plaza there are two deep square depressions that demarcate the foundations of the former World Trade Center towers. These two dark cavities seem to suck the warmth out of the surroundings, creating a feeling of extreme solemnity. They are scars on the surface of Manhattan Island, eternally carved into the hearts of New Yorkers. I am not sure how New Yorkers see them, but I feel these two scars have completely altered the atmosphere of the city.

While discussing my proposal, I naturally mentioned my critique of skyscrapers as being mere symbols of power and capital, lacking in humanity. As I spoke, I casually pointed out the window to the buildings of the rebuilt World Trade Center, some of them complete, some of them still under construction, and asked, "Will this really be the future of New York?" To my eyes, these buildings were no different from the formulaic skyscrapers that are mushrooming up in every second-tier Chinese city: enormous structures that maximize floor area and ground utilization, their lack of creativity concealed behind plate glass walls and a bit of perfunctory surface covering. After I finished introducing my work, I noticed the astonished expression on the face of the real estate developer. He protested that New York had regulations; reading between the lines, it was clear he felt New York's regulations were superior to those I might be familiar with. I suspect his conservative and rather arrogant attitude might be connected to the fact that he looks down on the Memorial Park every day. If the events of September 11 had not occurred, New York would certainly be considering works that would surpass the Twin Towers and represent a new vision for urban culture, rather than sinking into a state of morose conservatism. With the passage of time though, I hope New York will be able to rekindle its feisty spirit.

For a century humankind has realized its dreams and ambitions through the skyscrapers of Manhattan. These towers are a record of the transformations of society. They have progressed from objects of study, to objects of criticism, and finally to objects that pose a new challenge: Can we transform the city so that it becomes an expression of the basic relationship between people and nature? I feel this question will ultimately point the way to a new urban culture which, perhaps, will not be found in New York, but across the ocean in China.

The Floating Earth

A dish, like an expanse of earth, supporting life
We gaze towards the earth, but see only the world resting upon it
She seems a non-existent existence
A persistence
A boundless mirror
Home, city, limitless beneath our gaze
Layer upon layer, expansive
Unlimited possibility teeters on the precipice
All rooted in the silent, unchanging earth
Without her, there is no support, yet at any moment she may abscond
There is no love but for the blue sky

The Floating Earth,
Alessi product design model,
Ma Yansong, 2010.

Chapter 2

Nature
from a Human Perspective

"The human race's prospects of survival were considerably better when we were defenceless against tigers than they are today when we have become defenceless against ourselves."

——Arnold Joseph Toynbee

The Origin of Nature

A dictionary definition of the "world" might be: the sum of all objective phenomena in human society and in nature. To my mind, definitions like this betray a primarily Western worldview in which people and nature are placed in opposition to one another. The development of civilization is made equivalent to the reclamation of wilderness and its conversion into resources and wealth. However, even civilized humanity emerged from nature and ultimately, even though urbanized, continues to exist within it. Our inner core, our "human nature" still hints at our origins in the natural world. The depiction of landscapes in art is one way in which our longing for an emotional connection to the natural world is revealed. Within nature, we seek spiritual consolation and an affirmation of who we are. However, societies built upon the subjugation of nature have created a modern world in which a there is a rift between matter and spirit. The natural environment, plundered as a resource and further deteriorating with every passing day, is sending us warning signals in the form of storms of unprecedented strength, ecosystem collapse, and desertification.

In European and American cities, large-scale green spaces like Central Park are somewhat rare. While Central Park is notable for the high degree of planning and landscaping that went into its construction, other Western urban parks strive to maintain an untended feel, to replicate natural spaces within the city. Despite the variety of scales and approaches to urban green spaces found within Western cities, I find that they all are quite different to the parks and natural spaces I experienced growing up in Beijing.

Beijing's urban parks and green spaces lack Central Park's impressive sense of scale and the stark boundary between parkland and city. The parks I grew up with in the central districts of old Beijing were scattered with temples, pagodas, and pavilions, while our homes and buildings contained interior courtyards shaded by trees. Thus, my childhood seemed to take place in one enormous garden. Work, study, and life were all immersed in this verdant atmosphere. People lived in daily contact with nature. Perhaps because Beijing lacks a stark contrast between urban and natural space, I was never consciously aware of the existence of nature as a separate entity, just as you are not consciously aware of the existence of the air you breathe.

The hills and lakes of old Beijing are part of the city's original plan, and were designed according to the principles of feng shui, ecology, and water conservation. As an entirety, the city forms a vast landscape whose aesthetics are interwoven with its functionality. Roads, homes, schools, and offices all exist within it, giving residents the sense they are living in a scene from a Shanshui painting. Hangzhou and Suzhou are similarly beautiful, and express a similar harmony with nature. Works of literature describing the Beijing of my childhood frequently contain descriptions of this exquisite environment. These collective experiences and perceptions create a deep attachment to the city. It is heartbreaking that this traditional tapestry of urban life is fraying in so many Chinese cities, or, in some instances even being actively torn apart.

It was only after visiting a number of Western cities that I became aware of this special quality of certain East Asian cities. To this day, I still contemplate the question of why Western and Eastern cities were built so differently, even after taking into account their respective cultures' divergent views of nature. Later I discovered something interesting and noteworthy. At the Temple of Heaven in Beijing, one can find a number of ancient pine trees. Each is a protected tree, with a plaque to denote the year in which it was planted, the species, and its status as a cultural relic. In Western cities, I have never seen such a plaque on a tree. In France, I toured the gardens of the Palace of Versailles, where horticulturalists prune the trees into neat squares. When a tree eventually dies it will be replaced by another tree of the same species to preserve the symmetry of the garden. In the Temple of Heaven, individual trees are an integral part of cultural history, not just an interchangeable piece of landscaping. Ancient Chinese people saw a portrait of their own life and spirit reflected within each individual tree, each blade of grass, each mountain, river, and lake. We still yearn for a unity of the self with nature—not by merging the self into nature, nor by harnessing abstract spiritual energies, but by feeling a simple intimacy with our environment—to gaze upon an ancient tree and to feel, "I am in you, and you are in me."

In the Name of Ecology

"Ecological" is a very popular word these days. Broadly speaking, ecology is the study of the relationship between living things and their environment. Current usage of the word is a reflection of how post-industrial society uses every technological means conceivable to respond to the environmental crisis. Today's rapid expansion of eco-technology empowers conservation, environmental protection, and the improvement of ecological conditions. These aims are achieved via the use of technology to alter our physical environment. To my mind, ecological thinking addresses problems at a purely technological level, while nature itself transcends this level of consideration.

Recently I have been wondering, if a building or city minimizes environmental impact and conserves energy and resources, does this automatically make it "good?" Does this necessarily make it a place where we might choose to live? In New York, a recently completed high-rise bank was awarded the LEED platinum certification, one of the most stringent environmental standards in the US. The LEED standard requires meeting the highest benchmarks for environmental protection and energy conservation, which requires costly equipment and building materials. Examining this building from a design perspective, however, there is nothing to distinguish it from skyscrapers of the 1980s. The layouts of the lobby, elevators, and office spaces are all utterly conventional. This type of building is just a more advanced, more efficient version of the same Modernist machine. But a better machine is still just a machine, incapable of emotionally connecting to people.

This is not a question of advancing technology, because it is always in the nature of technology to quickly become outdated. "Good architecture" so designated for its technological advancement is really just an industrial product. It will quickly become obsolete and unsustainable. It only took a few years for the first generation of computers to become nothing more than museum exhibits. Yet a city or a building cannot be thrown away or placed in a museum. What buildings require is an enduring vitality.

I am often skeptical of energy efficiency and environmental protection methods that cost a fortune to implement. These methods are more rooted in the requirements of the supply chain than in people's true feelings for nature and the environment. While it is desirable to have the support of technology, technology should not supersede ethical and humanist concerns. Today, ecological architecture is stuck in a technical phase of development. However, it is not necessary to rely upon exceedingly expensive technology to build eco-friendly architecture. The precise definitions of "green" and "ecological" architecture are still under discussion, but they remain questions of material form. It is not nearly enough for a city to be highly efficient, energy conserving, and rational.

If we truly love nature, we should allow ourselves to experience it firsthand: let the sunlight shine on our bodies, let the wind blow in our faces, let our feet sink into the soil. We should not seal ourselves up within a mechanically controlled environment in which the temperature does not vary by even a single degree. I have always felt that sustainable development is actually a problem of awareness rather than a technical or industrial problem. The unfettered pursuit of comfort and high-tech solutions brings us no closer to a true appreciation of life. Those buildings and cities which have become a part of our cultural heritage have done so because they served as vehicles for the advancement of civilization and the human spirit. For example, do we appreciate classical Chinese gardens because they are "green architecture?" After all, they use recyclable, local, natural materials, and make use of natural ventilation and lighting. However, what makes them a treasured cultural heritage is their representation of a distinct worldview in which humanity and nature coexist in harmony, not the fact that they happen to meet certain ecological and environmental criteria.

Hongcun in southern Anhui province.

There are many examples of this within traditional Chinese architecture. The village of Hongcun is located at the foot of Mount Huangshan in southern Anhui province. (Hongcun is featured in Ang Li's film *Crouching Tiger, Hidden Dragon.*) There is a pond in the center of the village which plays an important role in the local ecosystem, aids in firefighting, and serves as a gathering place for the community. Due to its meticulous aesthetic, this pond has made Hongcun one of China's most iconic and picturesque villages. All of these outcomes were achieved without modern technology. Since the town and its layout originated from the natural environment, secondary environmental impact was never a concern, and a design that served the spirit of the community was achieved. The question Hongcun poses to us is how to define ecology in a way that does not view people merely as scientifically defined organisms. With all due respect to the technological innovations of ecological architecture, the only true sustainability lies in a building's spiritual and cultural significance for residents and the community.

The Shanshui View of Nature

Huangshan Mountain Village, Anhui province, Ma Yansong, 2009–2015.

Within the objectivity of the natural world there is no high and low. Desert, ocean, mountain, forest, and lake each have their own *raison d'être*. Nature does not require human validation. However, our existence is dependent on a kind of spiritual force which determines our relationship with the world.

The Shanshui worldview assigns a poetic significance to the relationship between man and nature which finds echoes throughout classical Chinese thought. Before China had written language, a culture of jade objects already existed. Excavating and polishing this hard, natural material is taxing work, but from these labors, a highly abstract art form was born. The natural patterns and textures of jade give each piece unique, subtle qualities for which it is admired. Acting as a microcosm of nature, jade endowed the Chinese people with a respect for the mysterious powers of the world around them, a respect that is transmitted not just through the sense of sight, but through touch as well. This is fundamentally different from the act of "seeing" that penetrates the entire system of Western art.

The culture of Jade speaks to a natural intelligence that transcends language, confirming the primal connection that existed between ancient people and their environment. This connection is best described as an ideal realm, a worldview that grew out of agricultural society, which saw humanity as arising from, and existing within, a state of symbiosis with obscure natural forces. The freedom that ancient Chinese people yearned for was not individual independence; rather it was a carefree enjoyment obtained by living in accordance with nature's flux. This contrasts with the desire to find sanctuary from the world found in Western religion, as well as the Western scientific project of reducing the natural world to rational principles. Ancient East Asian peoples entrusted their spiritual lives to the worldview of Shanshui, seeking the highest realms of thought and emotion within the relationship between humankind and nature. Generations of Chinese artists and poets labored in poverty to capture the spirit of this realm in their works. Their paintings and poems transcend the material qualities of their subjects. Mountain, tree, bridge, sky, cloud, and water merge into a singular mood, or vision. The connection between nature and the inner life of humanity was made manifest through paintings, poems, gardens, or even within a single bonsai tree. Each work is an entry point for discovering this connection, the ideal realm of Shanshui within us.

The fundamental principle in ancient Chinese architecture is the maintenance of the order that governs heaven and earth, and all existence. From the onset, architecture and environment were considered as a single entity. Respect and affinity for nature permeate the discipline at every scale, from the city as a whole, to every square inch of a house. Originating in nature, this design philosophy did not merely imitate the forms of the natural world. More importantly, it conveyed the inner experience of nature. There is a saying that "spiritual resemblance" is superior to "formal resemblance." Here, "spirit" represents the supremacy of the mind. The "ideal realm" of Shanshui exists within the reality of that spiritual resemblance, for which there is no fixed pattern or model. It is the expression of an artist's most profound experiences and thoughts, a mirror through which ordinary people might contemplate their lives. However, explaining Shanshui in its entirety is nigh impossible. It is more easily understood by contemplating an ink landscape on a scroll, or the wave-like patterns in a jade disc. Feeling transcends language. Feeling is truth.

Excerpt from Notes on a Small Rock Pool West of the Hill

by Liu Zongyuan, Tang dynasty

The Little Rock Fountain Journal, Ma Yansong, 2011.

120 steps westward from the hill we hear water beyond a bamboo grove. My heart delights at this sound so like the chiming of jade bracelets. We blaze a path through the bamboo and see a limpid pool below; no ripple mars its surface. Not far from the bank the rock bottom rises, emerging to form an island in miniature, with rugged highlands, peaks, and crags.

The pool holds over one hundred fish, all sliding unsupported through empty space. Sunlight shines through the pool, forming fishy shadows on the rock below. They hold still, then dart away, coming and going with ease, as if playing with those who have wandered here.

Gazing to the southwest, the creek meanders in Big Dipper curves, sinuous as a snake, slipping in and out of view. The opposite bank is jagged with boulders, a jumble of canine teeth obscuring the pool's source.

Sitting on the bank alone, isolated by walls of bamboo, the chill seeping into my bones, I feel a deep silence. One cannot linger in this cold and empty realm, so I take note of these things, then depart.

My companions: Wu Wuling, Gong Gu, and my younger brother Zongxuan. Two young brothers surnamed Cui also accompanied us, Shuji and Fengyi.

This famous piece of prose exemplifies the Shanshui view of nature: the delight and wonder at nature's unfolding beauty; the patterns that repeat at every scale, from rock to island, from pool to ocean; the joy of personal interaction with creatures and their environments; the stillness that lies both at the heart of nature, and within the human mind; and also those deep forces in nature that are incomprehensible and for which humanity remains in awe.

A Meeting Across Two Decades

"Does there exist a modern city that adapts itself to nature, a city that possesses the beauty of ink landscapes and verse, whose residents live in happiness?"

——Qian Xuesen

During my research I discovered that a renowned Chinese scientist had conceived a "Shanshui City" over twenty years before me. He was the father of China's "Two Bombs, One Satellite" program—Qian Xuesen. Qian proposed this idea during the early period of China's architectural modernization. In the 1980s and 1990s, large-scale, rectilinear, concrete buildings were sprouting up in cities throughout China. Qian noted skeptically, "Today I see all of these tall, rectangular buildings popping up, their exteriors like toy building blocks. Looking out from inside their rooms, you see a sea of gray, no green whatsoever, and not a single patch of blue sky. Will this really be the Chinese city of the twenty-first century?" Qian began to contemplate whether it would be possible to establish a new perspective on urban architecture and city planning using Shanshui and the environment as starting points. While respecting modernization in architecture, he hoped to endow the city with a natural spirit, cultural energy, and ideal living conditions.

In October 2010, I saw a large number of Qian Xuesen's handwritten letters on the subject of Shanshui cities while visiting the home of architect and professor, Gu Mengchao. On July 31, 1990, Qian Xuesen wrote a letter to the scholar Wu Liangyong. He had read about the rebuilding of Ju'er Hutong, a community in Beijing, in the *Beijing Daily* and *People's Daily* newpapers. This helped to catalyze an idea he had been toying with for some time. "In recent years, I have thought constantly about this question: Can the aesthetics of China's pastoral poetry, classical gardens, and landscape paintings be combined to create a 'Shanshui City?' Even as they lived separate from the natural world, residents would be returning to nature." The reason Qian Xuesen used the term Shanshui city instead of a more concrete description, such as "garden city," to express his idea, is that gardens were only one component of Shanshui culture. Shanshui implies a deeper understanding from which the aesthetics of Chinese poetry, garden landscaping, and painting are all derived. Not only did he coin this phrase, he also advanced a number of ideals for the design of Shanshui cities, such as the construction of tall buildings in irregular arrangements, as opposed to grids, interspersed with lofty trees. He said an "urban Shanshui" would require transplanting the principles of Shanshui painting into the realm of city planning while integrating modern architectural techniques with the knowledge of Chinese landscaping. His concept of "three-dimensional greening" involved not just the use of climbing plants, but also the installation of gardens and terraces with flowers and trees at various heights within the city. He envisioned ancient pines growing from the sides of high-rise buildings, simulating the natural scenery of revered peaks such as Huangshan or Mount Emei within an urban context.

Qian's Shanshui City was the only truly original urban planning concept to emerge in modern China, yet it was ignored for decades as the vacuous cities Qian warned about proliferated across China. How did this transpire?

At the time China had just entered a period of large-scale urbanization and speed was the priority. A rehashing of the North American urban model proved the simplest and fastest method, initiating a burst of razing, demolition, and construction in which towns grew into cities seemingly overnight. In hindsight it is clear that Qian Xuesen's ideas were far ahead of their time, foreseeing a future where aesthetic and spiritual concerns could be prioritized over speed and efficiency.

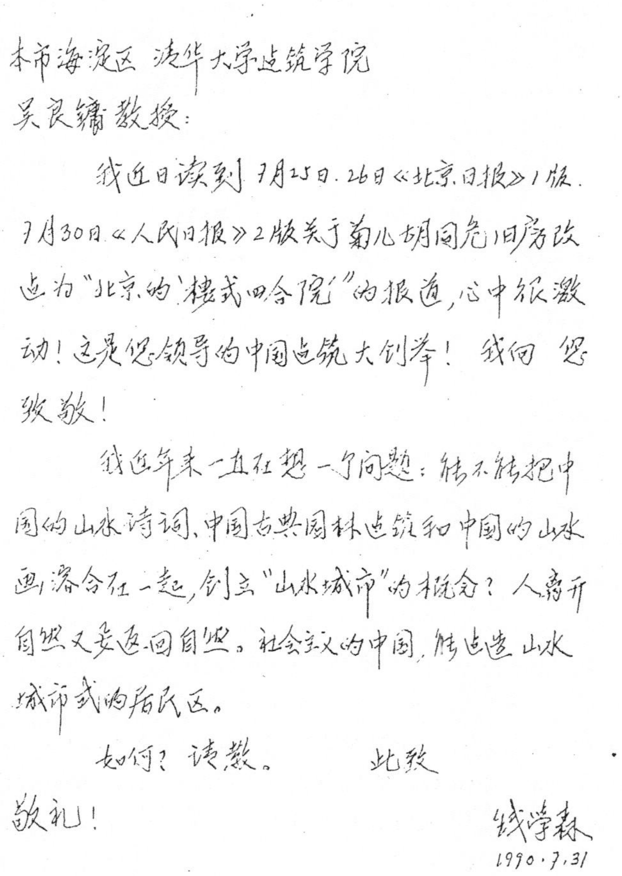

本市海淀区 清华大学建筑学院

吴良镛教授：

我近日读到7月25日、26日《北京日报》1版、7月30日《人民日报》2版关于菊儿胡同危旧房改造为"北京的'楼式四合院'"的报道，心中很激动！这是您领导的中国建筑大创举！我向您致敬！

我近年来一直在想一个问题：能不能把中国的山水诗词、中国古典园林建筑和中国的山水画融合在一起，创立"山水城市"的概念？人离开自然又要返回自然。社会主义的中国，能建造山水城市式的居民区。

如何？请教。 此致

敬礼！

钱学森

1990.7.31

Qian Xuesen's handwritten letter from July 31, 1990.

Returning to the Roots of Shanshui

I view Qian Xuesen's Shanshui City as an ideal for the architecture of inhabitancy. It reveals new directions for urban living and spiritual values based on the Shanshui view of nature. The concept of Shanshui he envisaged was not ecological, nor did it propose the maximizing of green space as in Le Corbusier's Radiant City. A city does not even necessarily have to be in a located within a picturesque natural setting to qualify as a Shanshui City. What Qian demonstrated was the possibility of a spiritual and emotional connection between humans and nature within an urban setting. To mend this long-severed bond, we urgently need to find a new method of reestablishing these connections.

Yet today we are still caught in a spiral of "instant-gratification" urbanization. Chinese cities appear prosperous, but the hazards of traffic congestion, air pollution, and social alienation remain. What has prevented our idealistic urban visions from becoming a reality? Perhaps the answer lies in our current notion of urban development and expansion, which runs counter to the historic spirit of Chinese cities that once defined Chinese urban life with their complete absorption with nature. People have become accustomed to the daily hardships of life in contemporary urban China. Consoled by the escapism of consumption, they no longer know how to find a path towards meaningful change.

Over the past thirty years, cities have mushroomed all across China. They are largely indistinguishable from one another and are completely lacking in character. Yet each city tries its utmost to project a proud and confident façade. Most of them boast a municipal government building modeled on the White House or a skyline reminiscent of Manhattan, signature buildings in which they take immense pride. For a country that is undergoing the largest-scale urbanization project the world has ever known, this is a rather unfortunate state of affairs. Due to a lack of conscientious urban planning, this global center of urbanization has become an empire of cheap imitation.

These copycat architectural productions have their origins in the eclecticism that pervades official ideology in China. After 1949, a group of Chinese architects returned from their studies abroad. Represented by Liang Sicheng, they tried to find a way to integrate Western architectural systems with traditional Chinese aesthetics. The "Ten Great

Buildings" built to commemorate the tenth anniversary of the founding of the People's Republic of China in 1959, including the Great Hall of the People, the National Museum of China in Beijing, and the Beijing Railway Station, are all representative works of this "proto-eclecticism." As products of the ideology of the time, each building's form reminds us of the fact that Beijing has always found it difficult to disengage culture from politics.

In the early 1980s, Western ideas flooded into China for the first time since before the Cultural Revolution. "Postmodernism" and "Deconstructivism," topics fervently discussed by Western architectural theorists, were only understood in China in a superficial manner. Sweeping across façades in every street and avenue in the city, these philosophical trends have left behind nothing but unintelligible fragments. This acquisitive collage hitches traditional culture to a crude system of industrial production, resulting in a chaotic urban landscape. I imagine this is not something that Qian Xuesen initially anticipated. After the era of the large-scale concrete box, architects, consumed by wealth and power, built cities devoid of any real cultural value. Since the construction spree of the 2008 Olympic Games and the 2010 World Expo, in all cultural endeavors, including architecture, we have moved towards a post-eclecticism that nevertheless remains defined by mixing and matching shallow interpretations of Eastern and Western cultural values.

Old Beijing, My Childhood

Bird's eye view of Beihai Park.

My discussion of Shanshui is rooted in my feelings towards nature—not the "pure" nature found outside the city, but the pockets of nature within the city. It is this "urban nature" that allowed me to transcend day-to-day reality and find a sense of belonging in the city.

My childhood was spent in Beijing's old, historic neighborhoods. In the center of every courtyard home was a large tree, and every part of our lives seemed to unfold underneath those trees. These courtyard trees were different from the trees that lined the street. People maintained an intimate lifelong dialogue with these trees; they were at the center of our family and community relationships. When I was younger, I would cross Jingshan Park and Beihai Park on my way home from school. In winter I would ice skate on the moat of the Forbidden City. In summer I learned to swim in the lakes of Shichahai and I caught fish off the Yinding Bridge. In retrospect, having these rolling hills and soothing bodies of water in such a large city was truly utopian.

Beijing is an epic city, constructed according to a grand order, yet replete with details that inspire our most subtle affections. As Lao She wrote, "The beauty of old Beijing lies in the gaps and voids between the buildings." It is these voids that establish a holistic relationship between the buildings, people, and nature. Having an urban center complete with hills, bodies of water, and open land sets Beijing apart from any other metropolis in the world. The historical "Eight Great Sights of Yanjing," which include Beihai Park, are a spiritual map of the city; its emotional calendar. These rich mythical landscapes are infused with the essence of ancient Chinese philosophy and aesthetics. They act as living canvases that can be experienced within the everyday lives of Beijing's residents, and treasured in their memories. This remarkable example of visionary urban planning is the physical interpretation of an idyllic natural world nurtured in the hearts of the Chinese people.

As a manifestation of the urban civilization of China's agricultural era, Beijing avoided the impact of twentieth century industrialization. Instead, the city leapt directly into its role as the political and cultural center of socialist China. Over the past five decades, each new iconic work of architecture heralded a new direction in the city's development. Unfortunately skyscrapers, cars, and gray skies have become Beijing's new defining features. Today's Beijing is a world apart from the old Beijing structured around order and nature. The original vision of the city has sadly been lost.

The *hutong* (narrow lanes, or alleys) and courtyard homes are the lifeblood of old Beijing, but today they are reduced to quaint amusements in a theme park. The ordinary people who have lived there for generations eke by without showers or bathrooms in their homes, or are banished to the margins of the city by forced demolitions. In the face of this urban atrophy and functional disorder, I believe it is necessary to make changes that are centered around the everyday lives of *hutong* residents. It is not necessary to rebuild wide swathes of the city; rather, small-scale interventions can be employed to improve living conditions and revitalize the sense of community in what remains of these neighborhoods.

Hutong Bubble No. 32, Beijing,
Ma Yansong, 2011.

In 2006, I conceived a "micro-utopian" project, which I called Hutong Bubble. These small-scale modules are inserted into traditional courtyard homes and can be used as studies, bedrooms, bathrooms, or for any other purpose suitable for a small space. My hope is that these "bubbles" will have the vitality of newborn cells, endowing old architecture with new energy. In this way, the program aims to revitalize the entire community though the transformation of a few components. A few years later, we constructed the first "bubble" in an old neighborhood of Beijing. This addition consists of a bathroom and stairs leading to a rooftop terrace, housed within an organic skin reminiscent of a single-celled organism. Its curving metallic exterior reflects the courtyard's ancient architecture, trees, and sky, thus blending into the environment. History, nature, and the future coexist within the dream-world reflections on the surfaces of these organic bodies.

Perhaps if we shift our attention away from large-scale, monumental architecture, we might be able to take a renewed interest in improving everyday living conditions in the city and rebuilding a community spirit.

Maintaining the concept behind old Beijing's urban structure does not necessarily entail replicating the old courtyard homes. Rather, within the high-density conditions that are the inevitable reality of future cities, we must consider how urban space can be shared and enjoyed, how to satisfy our yearning for harmonious interaction with nature, and how to preserve the integral spirit of older structures. All of these questions are related to our most fundamental human feelings, and determine whether residents can experience a sense of belonging within their urban environment.

Chapter 3

Towards a Shanshui City

A New Order

People often ask me why I design so many skyscrapers when it is clear that I have such great affection for Beijing's old courtyards. Can't we just build our city of the future with courtyard architecture? It's a question of density: with the vast scale of China's population and the sheer speed of its growth, if every household had a courtyard home, Beijing would be consumed by courtyards from the mountains to the sea. Dense, consolidated urbanization is the only way China can protect its natural resources and farmlands. This is a precondition for all debates on future urban inhabitation.

Today's megacities house populations of over ten million people. Due to the demands of greater efficiency and for the sake of the common good, these cities have given rise to a new form of society. I believe that people who live in dense urban areas have a special dignity. Megacities can facilitate the sharing of ideas and resources and provide a place where different cultures and values can coexist in previously unknown ways. In our current context, unlike at any other time in history, developing low-density, high-quality residences must be viewed as being extravagant and wasteful.

However, does a future without courtyard residences therefore imply an urban landscape devoid of greenery, and packed with oversized city blocks and skyscrapers? Where we cannot see the earth or trees, we cannot hear the birds, where we lack communal spaces. Our cities do not support the most basic needs of the human spirit—to say nothing of their lack of character. Our discussion of Shanshui comes at a time when the modern city is facing an environmental crisis. As we probe the relationship between humanity and nature, our research ought to target problems facing large, high-density cities. Furthermore, this research should not only be limited to the cities of East Asia.

Shanshui is a worldview defined by the ancient Chinese understanding of nature. It is an ideal environment that exists in perpetuity within the psyche of the Chinese people, available to all. It embodies a certain understanding of nature, crystallized from cultural memories of interactions with the natural world. It is an emotional experience that connects us to our environment. It is not merely mountains, or rivers, or foliage, or any specific natural object. As the process of urbanization

unfolds, so our longing for nature grows stronger. Thus, we begin to endow nature with social and cultural attributes.

The Shanshui City is a new mode of urban civilization centered on the relationship between humanity and nature. It requires the establishment of a new order in urban and residential planning which necessitates new priorities to define our urban ambitions. We cannot allow ourselves to be trapped in the infinite loop of technological development, with each new invention solving the problems created by the last. Instead, we must create a new holistic habitat for life and for the spirit. The facilities of the city should be defined with respect to how we would like to live and not vice versa. Residents should not be forced to accommodate a cold, abstract machine, lest our cities be overcome with antipathy and crisis. If we take the individual emotional response as primary, the result will be a humane and open city. While supporting the commons, the city should also reflect the great heights of artistic achievement and thought, just as the finest cities and gardens of ancient China were often the result of the collaboration of great thinkers and artists. In the realm of Shanshui City, art and thought are not mere luxuries; rather, they are directly integrated into everyday urban life.

To build a Shanshui City is to build a new spiritual homeland. Plans for such a city should abide by the following ideas and principles:

1. Mountains are not mountains; water is not water
2. Gaps and voids
3. Borrowed scenery
4. Green space ratios in space
5. Urban spaces on a human scale
6. Invisible transportation

1. Mountains Are Not Mountains; Water Is Not Water

Mountains: the most imposing physical presence within the natural world, they have compelled human cultures to assign them a range of symbolic meanings. In traditional Chinese culture, the mountain is not merely what one sees; it has more to do with the way one imagines the world. A mountain is not reduced to its objective physical existence, nor is a river just a vein of water that we give a name; rather, they constitute

Ice Ink, Ma Yansong, 2006.

Ice Ink, Ma Yansong, 2006.

that realm of thought which is traditionally expressed through ink landscape paintings, or Shanshui. For many centuries Chinese artists have used the act of representing nature to capture emotional qualities. They have borrowed the idealized forms of nature metaphorically to serve as symbols of the human spirit. Shanshui constitutes a realm of artistic expression that cannot ultimately be transmitted by written text.

Water: the most common substance on earth. It lacks constrained form, changing with external conditions. As the origin of life, water can be found almost everywhere. Whether as minute drops of rain or the vast ocean, it is inextricably tied to the fate of human civilizations. In the ancient East, water was not only understood biologically, according to its role in supporting organic life. Water was further seen as an illusory substance imbued with philosophical significance, able to embody the primordial forces of Yin and Yang. Through the observation of water, the ancient Chinese learned to see a world of deeper significance, to look beyond mere form. Bruce Lee once said that water embodied his understanding of Chinese martial arts: strength within suppleness.

Water in Shanshui paintings is most often portrayed with negative space. Though the painter does not draw waves or ripples, and certainly not a reflected image as one might see in a Western landscape painting, we can still nevertheless sense the presence of water in the painting. This negative mode of expression effectively conveys an imagined space in which poetic resonances can reside. When we say, "water is not water," we refer to that which transcends the physical attributes of water. This allows for the spiritual reshaping of the object, thus shattering our common conception of water and introducing us to water as a component of the realm of thoughts and ideals.

In architecture, this realm is grasped by refining an emotional response to the world down to its essence, and capturing it in physical form. It is a thing that cannot be expressed through a text or a diagram alone. No amount of describing or expounding can convey its inner meaning. The initial feeling of the architect is disproportionate to the enduring sense of time realized through the work of architecture, but it nonetheless plays a formative role in realizing the work.

Many Modernist architects pursue a kind of logical rationality, a perfection that is self-evident. This is not my method. I hope that my work remains somewhat indistinct, so that its essence is only glimpsed; perhaps sensed subliminally rather than overtly seen.

When discussing Louis Kahn's Salk Institute some have argued that trees should have been incorporated into the courtyard to reflect the central motif of nature. I have even heard that Kahn, himself, struggled with this question. I believe, however that the dramatic spatial effect of the site would have been diminished by the introduction of trees. Here visitors can enter into a dialogue with the sky and the sea, with limitless space and time. Only in this way can the architecture transcend the merely physical and evoke the sense of an ideal realm. It is for this reason that this masterpiece has been deemed a sacred space. Similarly, Shanshui is not a question of whether to plant trees or not. Green architecture is really only a technological concept, whereas the ideal realm of Shanshui is based on emotion and feeling. It is a state of mind rooted in the feelings evoked by the ocean, the desert, mountains, and lakes—but what can be said of the feeling evoked by a city composed of nothing by towering skyscrapers?

Contemporary urban planning is dominated by technological benchmarks and standards; the ephemeral realm of feeling and emotion does not enter into the discussion. Each time we temporarily leave the city and return to nature's embrace, we see mountains and water in their true forms. They are pregnant with meaning and significance, essential components of the realm of Shanshui. When we return to the city, there is no way for us to bring these landscapes back with us. But is there some way we can recreate the poetic resonance of Shanshui within the landscape of urban life? Can we transform human-made cities into environments that take on a holistic significance? Can we use such a city to reconstruct the emotional dialogue between humankind and nature? It is futile and impractical to merely replicate elements of nature within the city; urban spaces cannot simply be occupied by wilderness. The Shanshui City pursues the artistic principle that "mountains are not mountains; water is not water." It differs from the ecological concepts of green space and drainage systems. At its core, it requires modeling the ideal city of our imagination on internalized scenic forms, because what we see is not just mountains and water, but ourselves resonating within the landscape of the mind.

2. Gaps and Voids

Let us return to the passage from Lao She quoted above: "The beauty of old Beijing exists in the gaps and voids between the buildings, where trees grow and birds live. There is no need for the buildings to display themselves."

From top to bottom, the order of the old Beijing city center enabled a high degree of freedom within a unified whole. As the grey backdrop to the city's imperial architecture, *hutong* courtyards were the soil that nourished Beijing's cultural heritage and lived history. These courtyard spaces are rich and varied, full of "gaps and voids," walkways and breezeways between buildings. Their fundamental orientation is towards people. Through them, residents experience nature, life, and the changing of the seasons. They differ from modern parks and squares in their intimate connection to individual life and emotion. Humans and nature coexist within them as a matter of course. In ancient East Asian cities, architecture nearly vanishes within this total infusion of nature. The courtyard is the typological form that permits this sublimation of architecture by nature. The Chinese view of "quality of life" is mountains, waterways, openings, and emptiness all present within an urban landscape. This is what sets Beijing apart from other cities. This is what used to nurture the city's soul.

The philosophy and theoretical concept underpinning the urban plan of old Beijing does not differ from that of a garden, and a garden does not differ from a bonsai tree. Methodologies may vary, but the underlying philosophy holds true at all scales of application. In all domains we must pay attention to the relationship between negative space and the whole. Open spaces should form the core of urban planning, rather than being viewed as the space that is left over. Even as our future cities expand, we must continue in the tradition of ancient urban planners who saw "gaps and voids" as the spaces where the relationship between humankind and nature was nourished at a variety of scales. This will do more than provide space for trees and life to flourish; this will also provide space for the city's soul to take root, for a sense of freedom to flourish. New developments need not be overwhelming; they can be counterbalanced by everything we choose not to construct. When the logic of East Asian landscapes and gardens with their voids and open spaces becomes the core of city planning, we can build more than an environment which merely satisfies the functions of daily life—we can

Ordos Museum, Ordos,
Ma Yansong, 2005–2011.

build a holistic environment that invites us to take refuge from the mundane demands of life.

In some projects, I have begun to imagine a kind of "floating courtyard" structure. By stacking entire courtyard neighborhoods above one another, we can create structures that are perforated by an organic network of three-dimensional gaps and voids. These mountain-like stacks allow for the continuous merging of interior and exterior space in all dimensions, creating a hanging garden within the city. This form of micro-Shanshui may provide a means to extricate ourselves from the cold drabness of the modern city and revive the desirable characteristics of traditional residential spaces. It is a model that can be adopted gradually. Each new building can accommodate itself to and interact with existing structures and voids, until eventually this new model of architecture becomes integral to the basic urban fabric of the city.

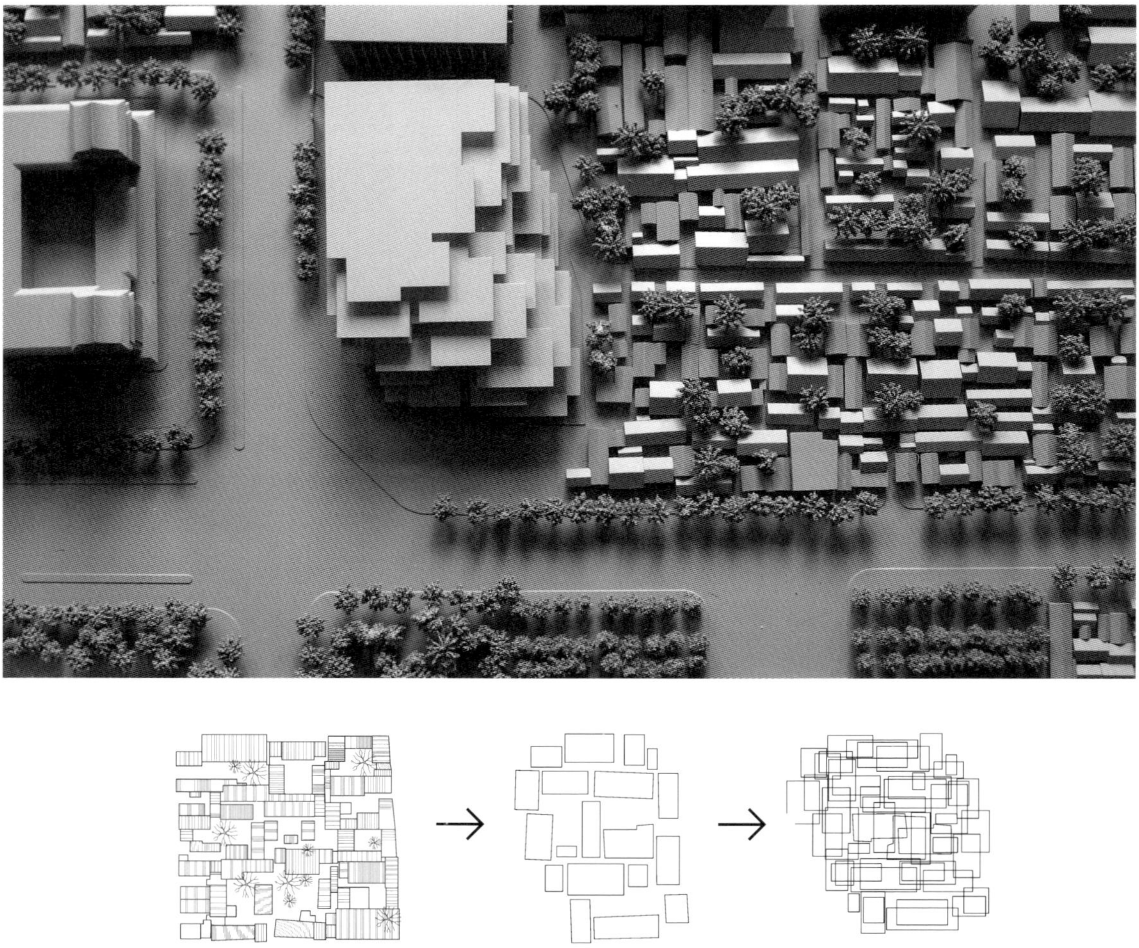

Guardian Art Center, Beijing, Ma Yansong, 2008.

3. Borrowed Scenery

Yinding Bridge, Beijing.

Borrowed scenery is a technique in traditional Chinese garden design. It is a concept that operates on two levels. The garden incorporates the surrounding scenery, while also becoming a piece of the larger landscape. Landscape and garden each merge into the other.

Take Beijing's Yinding Bridge on Houhai Lake as an example. It is a short pedestrian bridge; on its western side is the long and narrow Houhai Lake. If you were to stand above the arch of the bridge and look westward, you would see the mountains and their reflection in a long stretch of water. At that moment you would become aware of the fact that you were standing in the center of the city. These dramatic effects are meticulously planned, taking into account the movement of the visitor within the garden while employing both the surrounding environment and distant landscape as vistas.

In contrast, buildings in modern cities are like machines built only to maximize their disparate benefits. They are for the most part divorced from nature and the surrounding environment. As these buildings fill the city, they create a "concrete jungle." Their problem is not the choice of their materials, rather it is the simpl crudeness they embody with their total disregard for the holistic environment. This fact is easily revealed by the ever-increasing size of urban structures that dominate city skylines and the inhabitants of cities alike. Such eyesores cannot easily be overlooked.

Is it possible for contemporary urban planning to take the creation of a holistic landscape as its core mission; to consider large-scale architecture as a component of the greater environment? Can the city become a three-dimensional landscape appreciated by those who live and work within it? The city skyline, an elevator, a highway ramp, a wall, an elevated platform—all these elements should integrated into the urban fabric. Just as with the Yinding Bridge which serves an architectural function, but whose genius lies in its ability to enhance our appreciation of the larger environment. This is the sort of detail that infuses the atmosphere of a city with subtle charm.

4. Green Space Ratios in Space

Everyone enjoys green spaces, but in modern high-density cities, every inch of space is carefully budgeted and accounted for. Under these constraints, the relaxing spaces provided by parks, courtyards, and outdoor terraces have become increasingly rare in China.

Every time I have tried to incorporate courtyards, gardens, and terraces into three-dimensional spaces, or green spaces on the upper floors of high-rises, rather than leaving them on the ground, I have faced endless controversy. Today's architectural regulations stipulate that these kinds of green spaces and communal spaces reduce the total commercial floor space of the building. These regulations are a major hindrance to the reform of high-rise architecture. The developers of high-risers are concerned with maximal usage rates, forcing architects to forgo notions like three-dimensional gardens and open public spaces.

New planning regulations should adopt a three-dimensional perspective. A planar city must have at least 30% green space by land area, but for a three-dimensional city this figure is not nearly high enough. When a building's gross floor area is 300%, 500%, or an even greater percentage of its site area, the area given over to green spaces should also increase proportionately. What is required is a three-dimensional green space ratio based on total floor area, rather than on site area. We must use the concept of three-dimensional gardens in design strategies for the city of the future to avoid exacerbating trends of congestion and inhumane living conditions. In future urban planning, elevated green spaces, elevated public spaces, and aerial connections should become basic criteria for urban design, and should receive corresponding regulatory support.

Of course, the design of these aerial landscapes should abide by the principles laid out above. Architects must strive to invoke an intimate connection to the elements of the natural world and elevate humanity's relationship to nature. The elegantly twisted form of the Greeting Pine at the peak of Huangshan provides a natural example of greenery suspended at altitude, surrounded by hard vertical surfaces of stone. It enhances the atmosphere of the peak, and has enticed countless visitors to make the long climb to admire its solitary, wistful presence. The Greeting Pine enduring role in the hearts of visitors has given rise to numerous literary tributes by ancient literati; it has become a poetic symbol for the larger natural world.

Via Boncompagni Housing,
Rome, Ma Yansong, 2010–2016.

5. Urban Spaces on a Human Scale

The spirit and values of the city are in a constant state of flux, from cities designed around religious sites, to cities designed around monuments to capital, and finally to cities designed for humanity. Externally, this is embodied by changes in the scale of the city. In the modern city, people are dwarfed by the sheer scale of the immense skyscrapers, public squares, and wide avenues. Buildings continue to grow larger, while we remain the same size. We are overwhelmed in the face of this vast scale, forced into numb submission.

Would it be possible to transform the scale of high-density cities to create the sense of wellbeing and comfort found in small and medium-scale urban spaces, streets, and landscapes? In ancient cities the abundance of pedestrian roads, small-scale gardens, and outdoor public spaces fostered a feeling of community. Perhaps our colossal buildings can be embedded within pedestrian-scale neighborhoods? Or could their size somehow be concealed so that they don't subsume adjacent urban spaces? The goal should be the elimination of the sense of estrangement between people and large-scale architecture by blending the buildings into their surroundings, so that they become pleasing components of an inviting landscape.

This is a challenge that requires careful consideration with respect to both the two-dimensional masterplan and three-dimensional urban space. I believe that this transformation can begin with the density of the city. Scattering the largest structures could reduce density and balance the city's visual landscape. At the same time, elevating medium and small-scale communal spaces within the three dimensions of the city could create a more amicable human interface for larger structures, so that they no longer tower over the city's inhabitants.

6. Invisible Transportation

The modern city is frequently planned around traffic routes and vehicles. Our grids of streets and highways treat transportation as the primary structuring principle of the city. This mode of urban planning has given rise to a series of problems. Excessively wide roads divide the city into isolated islands. Problems of scale, density, and layout

Nanjing Zendai Himalayas Center, Nanjing, Ma Yansong, 2012–2017.

are amplified by prioritizing vehicles over people. High-density buildings combined with poor pedestrian access force us to become more dependent on cars even though theoretically they are not necessary in high-density areas.

In a city designed around people, the surface should be reserved for pedestrians and low-speed transportation. High-speed transportation networks should be kept underground whenever possible, freeing up the earth and sky to harbor a more humane pace of life. Slow traffic lanes and pedestrian walkways can replace expressways and congested avenues. The surface of the city should rightfully be the domain of urban Shanshui. The elimination of motorways and arterial roads frees up space for communities to organically blend into one another, rather than be defined by the strict lines of the city grid. I call this principle "invisible transportation."

There is a deliberate curve in the road at the intersection of Jingshan Front Street and Wenjin Street on the northwest corner of the Forbidden City in Beijing. It is difficult to navigate this area, and cars have to pass by slowly. Judging its design from a purely functional standpoint, it could be seen as a failure. However, it also affords iconic views of scenic Beihai Park and of one of the magnificent corner turrets of the Forbidden City from across a moat. As you traverse by foot along the bend, you are rewarded with vistas that would have been impossible if transportation concerns had been prioritized over aesthetic ones. For its city center, Hangzhou in Zhejiang province had roads built beneath West Lake to protect the scenic area around the lake. This preserved the idyllic views known as the "Ten Scenes of West Lake," whose long history makes them a cultural institution in themselves. When the structure of urban space is designed around the city's scenery rather than the efficiency of transportation, the city can be transformed into a landscape expressive of the values of Shanshui.

Hiding transportation beneath the surface naturally requires greater investment, as subterranean spaces have to be excavated. Perhaps the tools and methods of transportation will need to be transformed as well. In exchange for this investment, however the city's surface can revert to a human scale, freeing up the structures of urban spaces to meet human needs. To my mind this is certainly a worthwhile trade-off. New York's High Line Park, built on a disused elevated rail line, has become one of the most dynamic public spaces in the city. It is a compelling symbol for the shift away from the transportation needs of industrial civilization and towards the essential relationship between people and their natural environment.

Chapter 4

The Future

The dystopian city of the future depicted in science fiction films is often a chaotic jumble of industrial age ruins, an ecological disaster where blue skies are have long been forgotten. I hope these cinematic visions turn out to be a warning and not a prophecy. The rapidly mushrooming urban centers of China are a super-lab for research on the future of the city. This presents an opportunity. This stage of urban civilization in China will be closely scrutinized, with the potential to uncover new possibilities. When China's current campaign of dynamic urbanization is finally over, nothing would be more regrettable than if no constructive ideas emerged from this period of frenetic development.

It is extremely difficult to discuss ideals in today's pragmatic China, though it remains important to do so. The ideal of the city has nothing to do with abstract GDPs or capital-producing CBDs; rather, it concerns the pursuit and creation of a holistic urban spirit. This spirit should lie at the foundation of urban development.

Shanshui City is an ideal for the future of inhabitation. Visionary depictions of an ideal future city were common during the early stages of urbanization in the West. Elevated mass transit, skyscrapers, towering chimneys—the ideals of the previous age have gradually become today's reality. We need to reawaken this longing for the future.

A vision: The skies of the future are blue and the cities are green. The ideals of ancient civilization have been restored. Cities embody a traditional worldview where humans and nature exist in harmony. Urban planning is pedestrian and community-focused. Architecture is integrated into beautiful environments, no longer hemmed-in by congested motorways. Buildings nestle into natural scenery, accentuating the urban landscape: an office high-rise is more like a mountain than a gleaming tower; terraced residences are punctuated by hanging gardens, cascading waterfalls, bamboo groves, and pools of water; every few floors, trees and open-air communal spaces emerge from the undulating forms of high-rises. Unassuming in character, the buildings of this city do not rely on expensive materials and technology for their appeal. Instead they emphasize the aesthetic mood evoked through the interaction between architecture and environment. In this atmosphere, residents have space to seek their innermost being. The dignity of life and the harmony of the community are restored to the city.

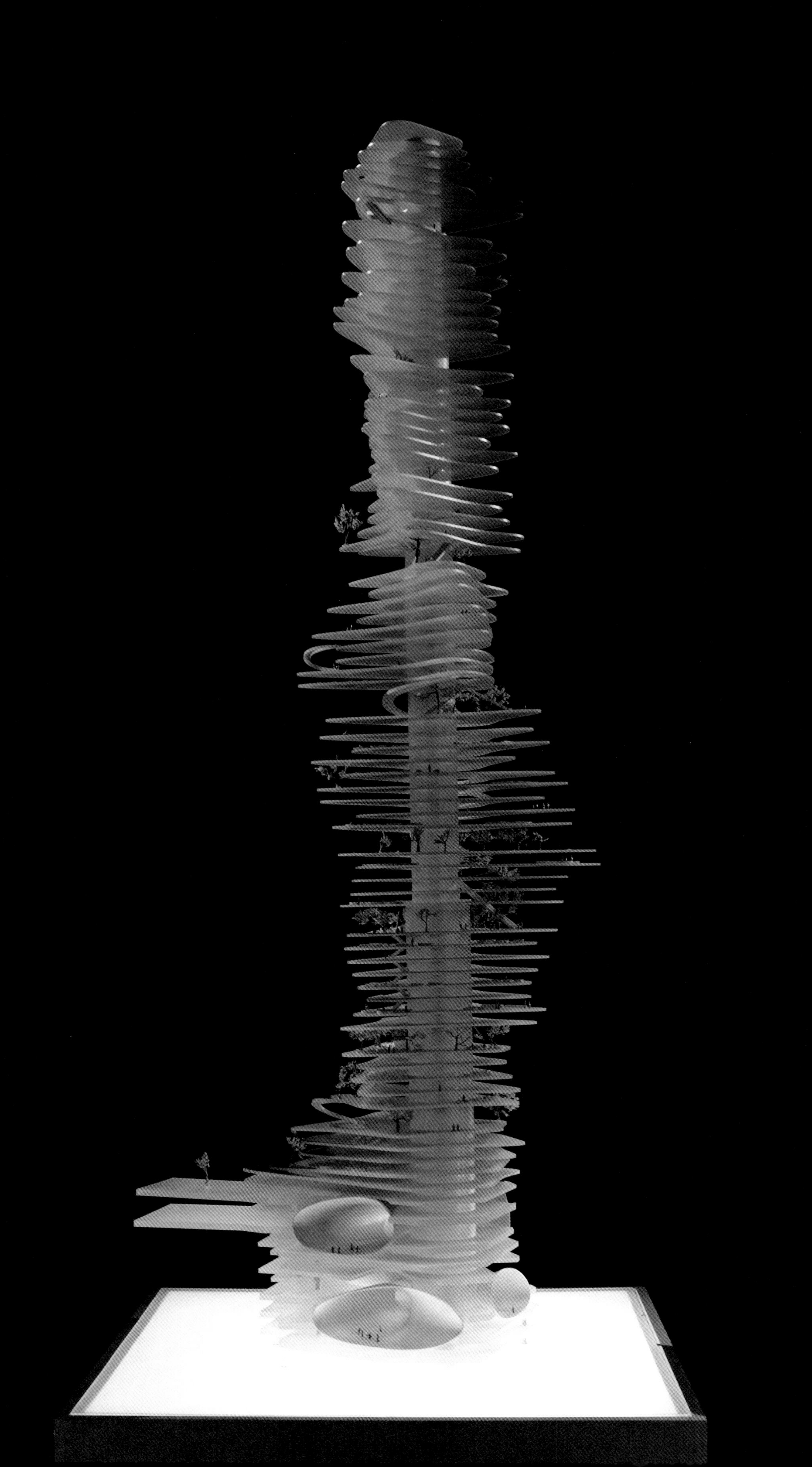

The Shanshui City is an organic entity whose core is the emotional connection between people and nature. It may take the form of mountains, water, or clouds—or it may not. Its form emerges from the refinement of an inner emotional resonance; there can be no formal template. The intention of the Shanshui City is to evoke principles of life and nature. It is guided by emotional concerns. It is a city where the harmonious interplay of human activity and natural growth is encouraged; a city that evokes the aesthetic resonance of an ink landscape, or the layered subtlety of an ancient poem; a city illuminated by the radiance of the human spirit. When we imagine the possibilities of the city of the future, we are taking the first steps towards their realization. "Towards a Shanshui City" is the process of sublimating the material into the spiritual. It is the path by which our humanity is restored. Through it we mark the beginning of a new historical process. It is the calling of our time.

The Shanshui City is an open-ended mode of thinking with the potential to change the course of urban planning and construction in China, and initiate a new era of urban culture. Perhaps this will be China's contribution to the world, the fruit of this ancient nation's accelerated age of urbanization.

Urban Forest, Chongqing, Ma Yansong, 2009.

Nanjing Zendai Himalayas Center

Nanjing, China

2012–2017, Under Construction

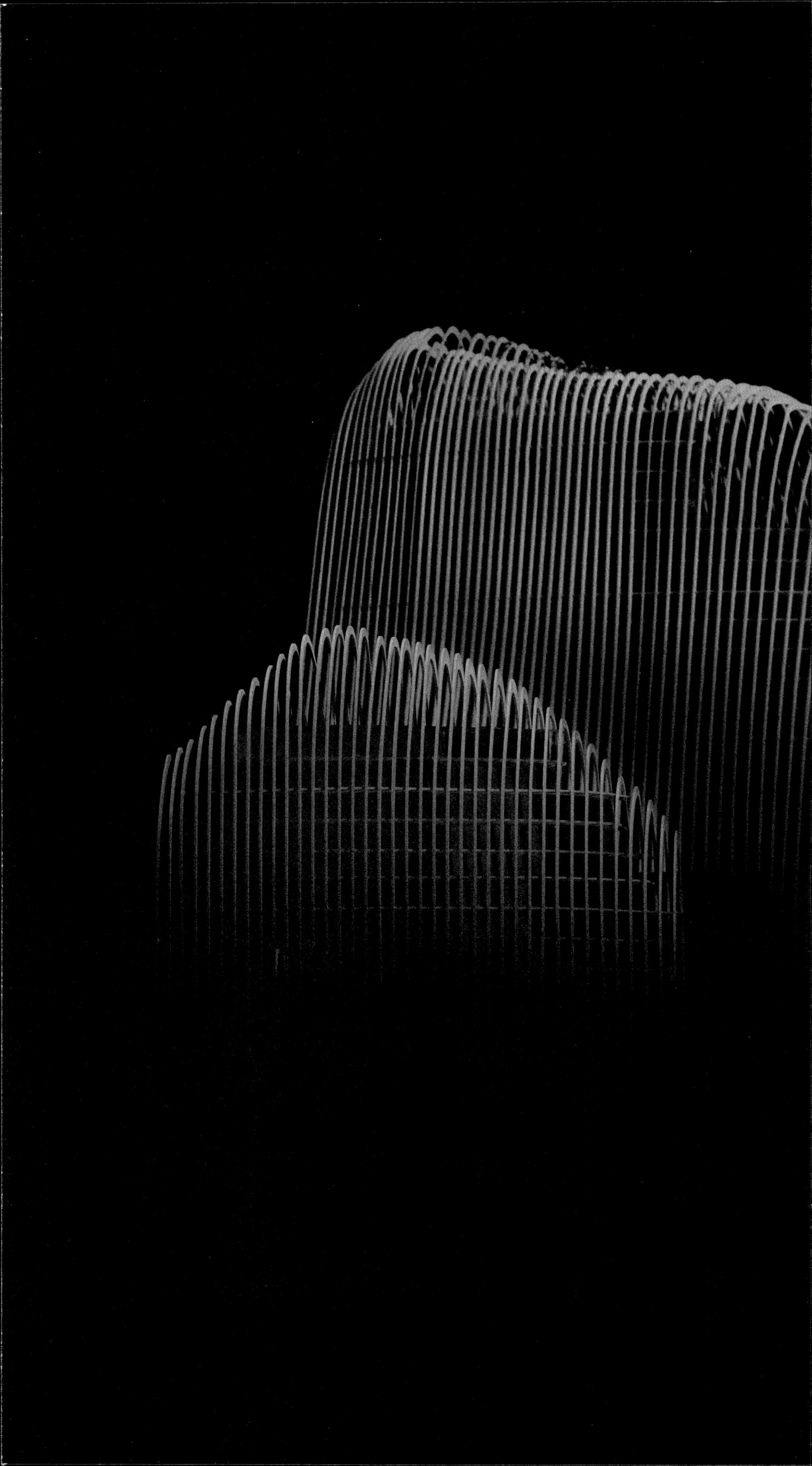

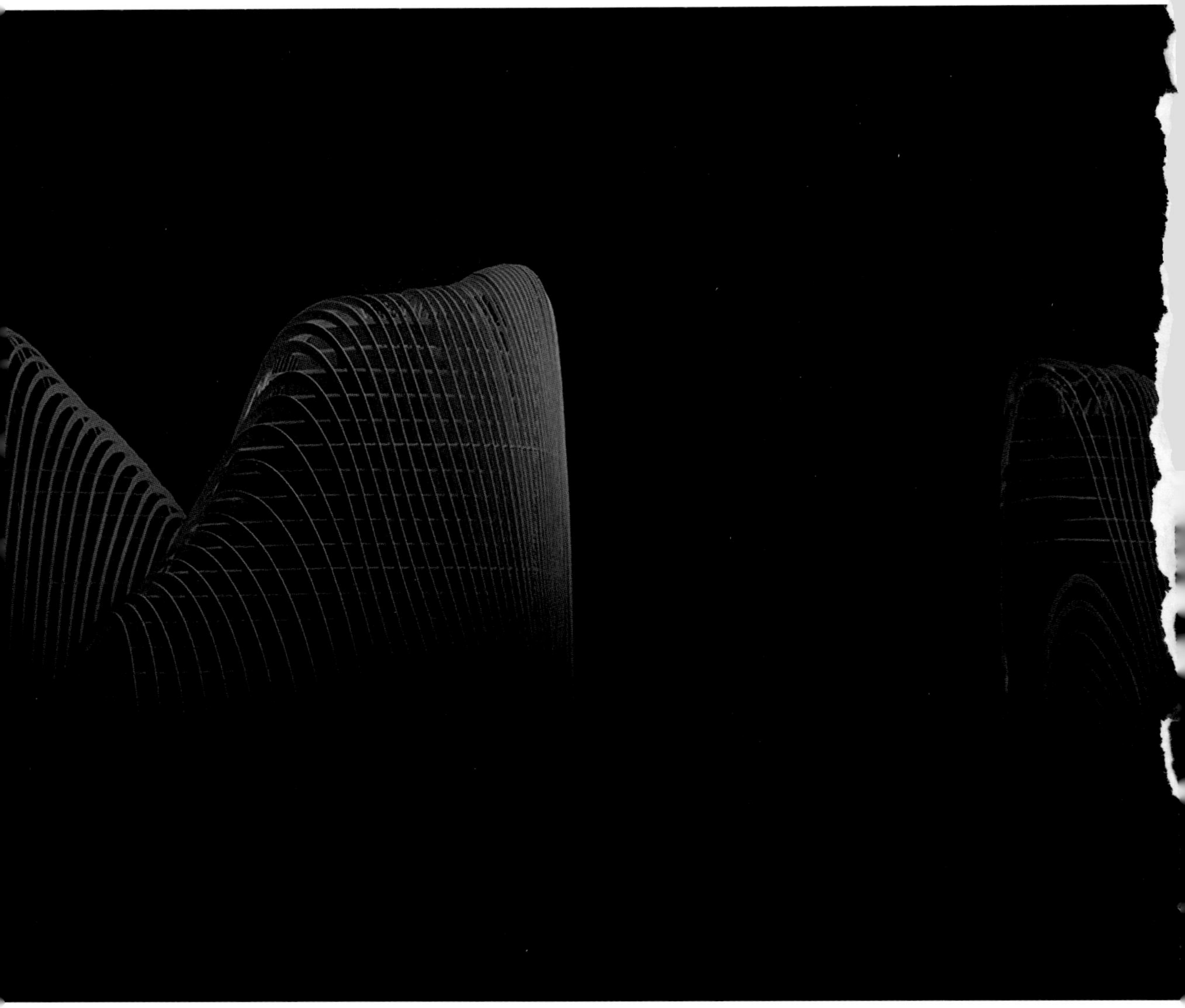

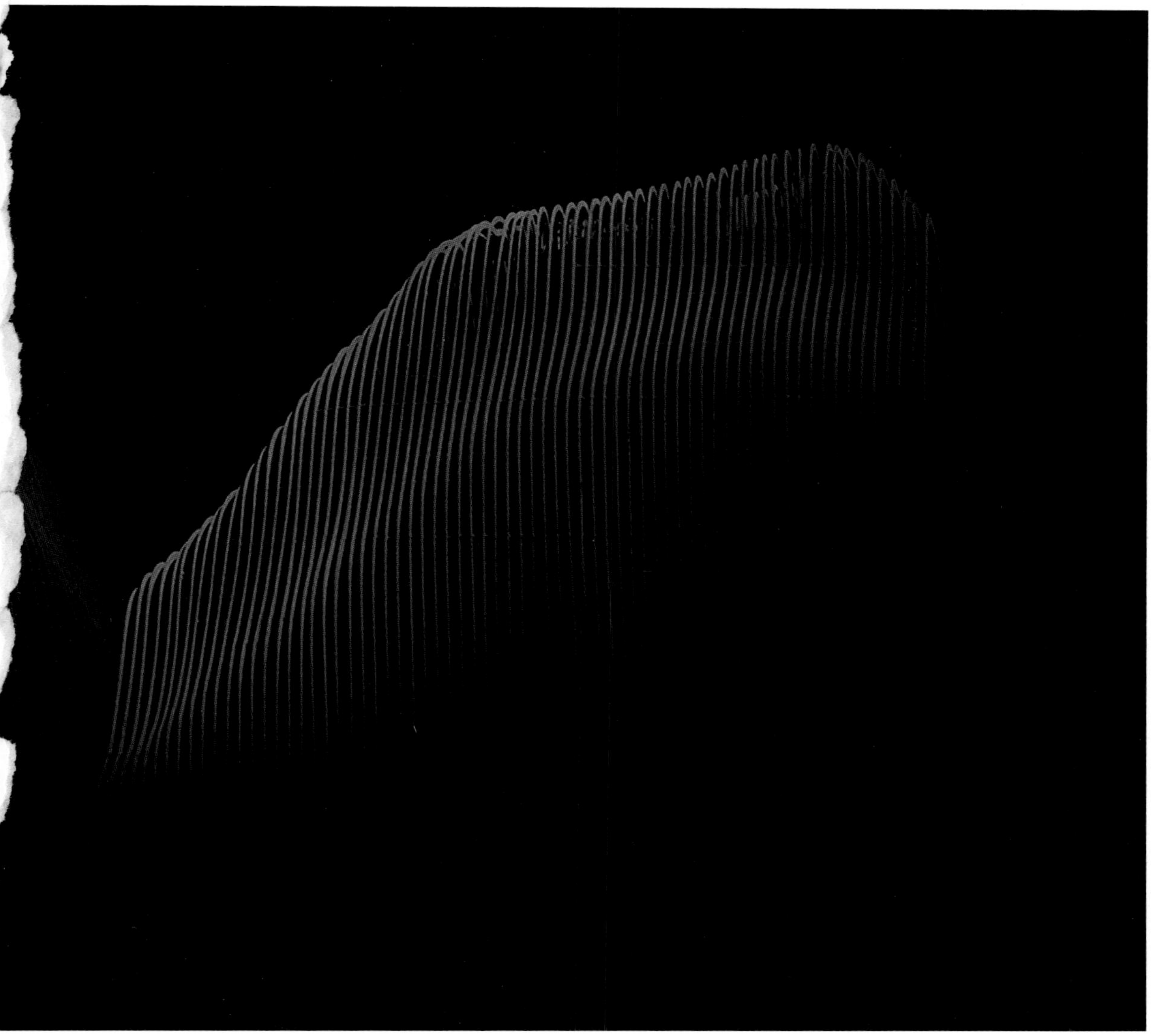

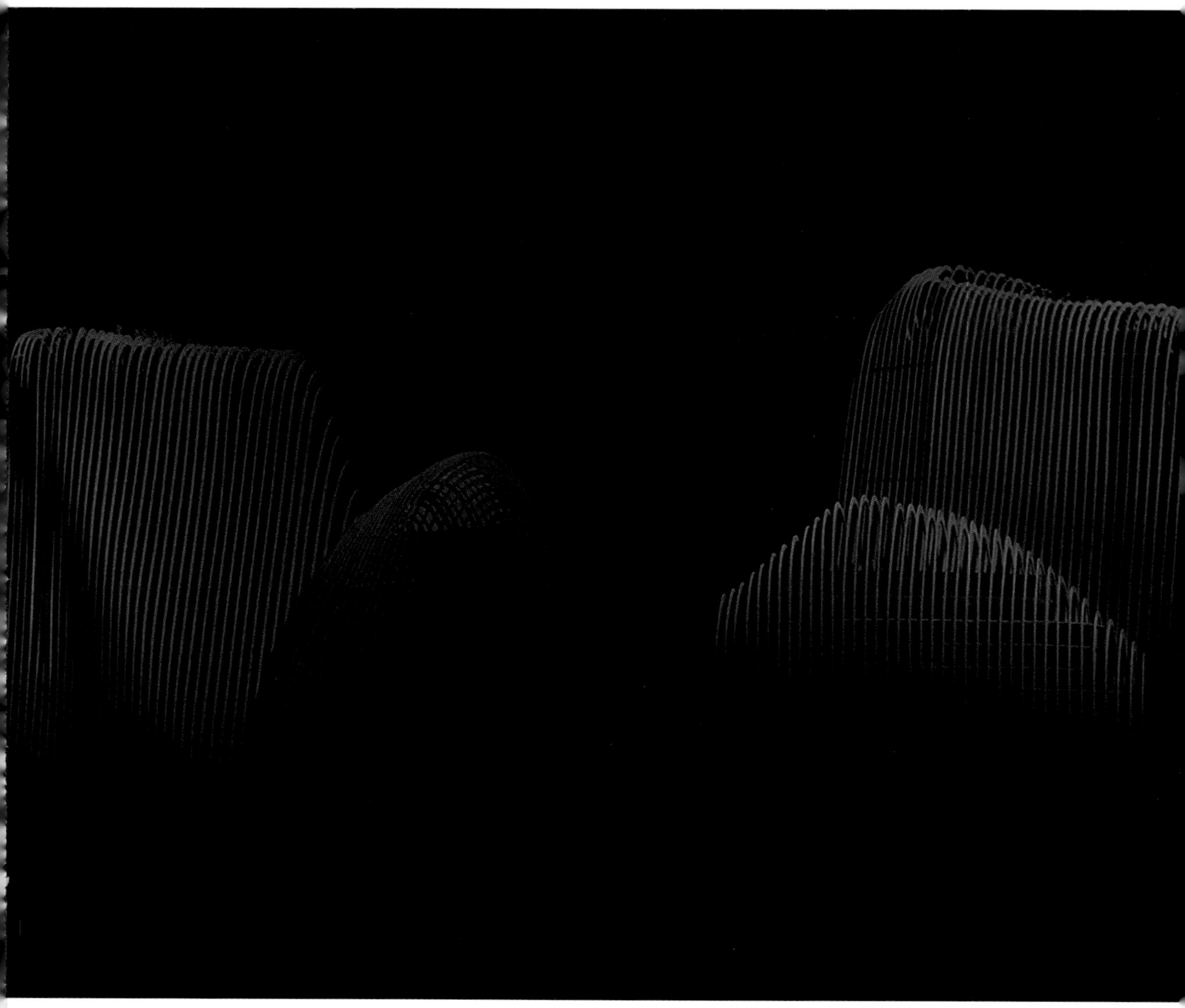

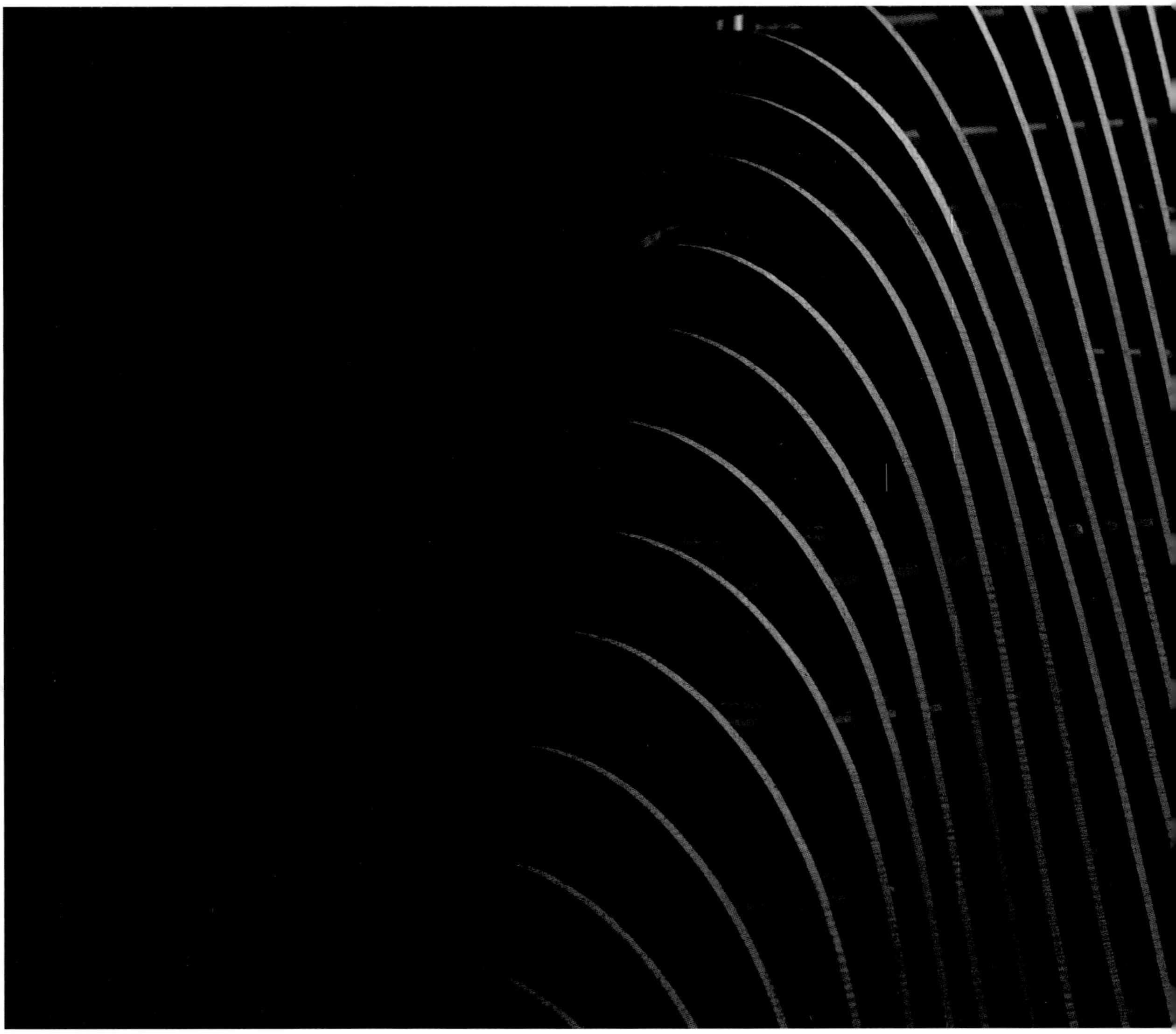

Clusters of towers form lofty peaks amid winding water.
In continuous transformation, sinuous forms manifest their subtle rhymes.
This architectural experiment melds modern urban life
with the emotional resonance of Shanshui.
Through this work, the modern city hearkens back to
an ancient Eastern intimacy with the natural world.

Chaoyang Park Plaza

Beijing, China

2012–2016, Under Construction

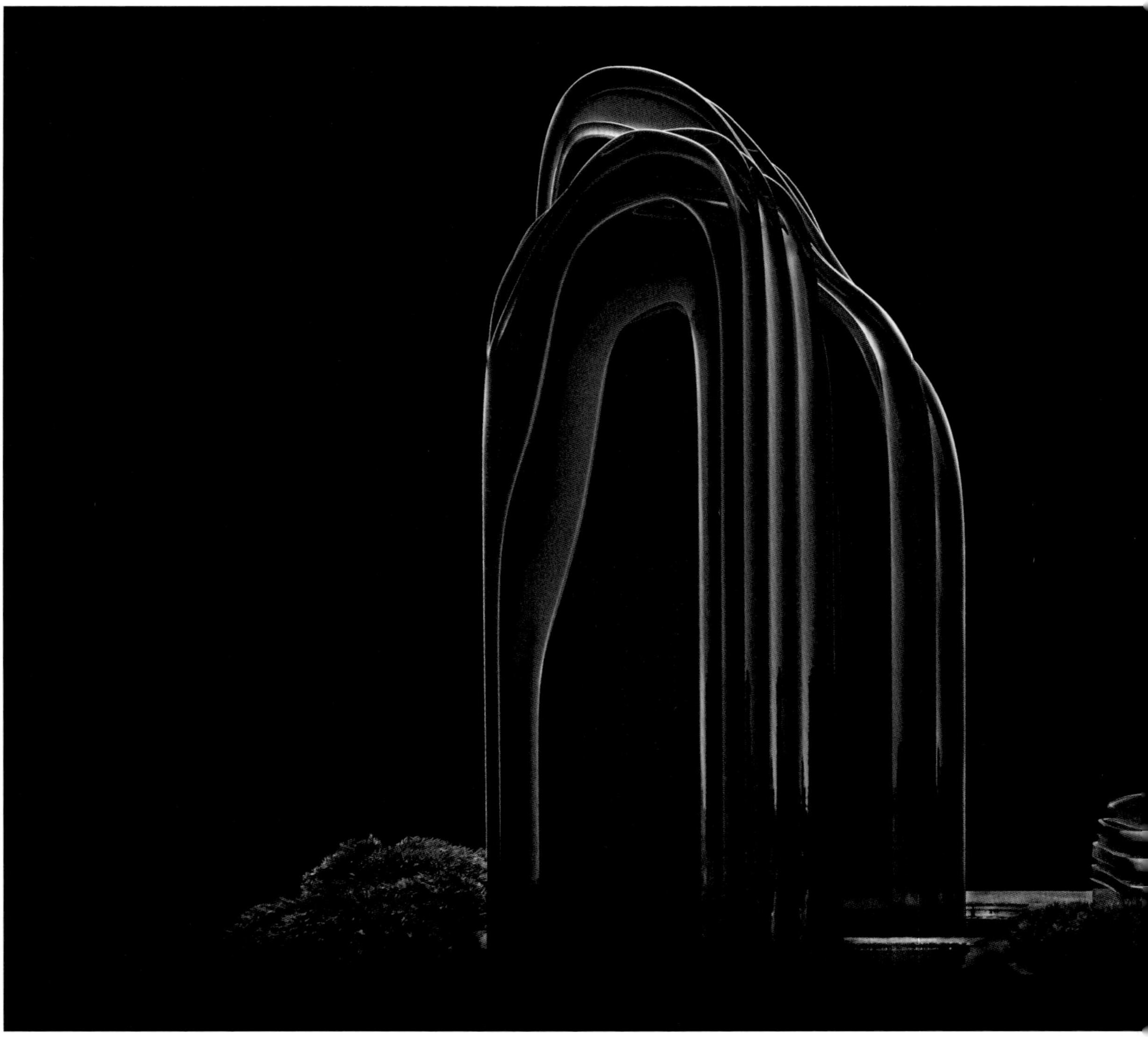

This impressionistic space resulted from restoring urban structures to the domain of nature.
Architectural clusters unflold according to the natural order of Shanshui.
The towers and nearby lake complement each other in a dance of reflected scenery.
A harmonious balance of soaring heights and intimate proportions defines this urban oasis.
Variations in density and height give the impression of
living architecture growing within a natural environment.
Artifice and nature are juxtaposed to call forth an effortless vision of Shanshui.

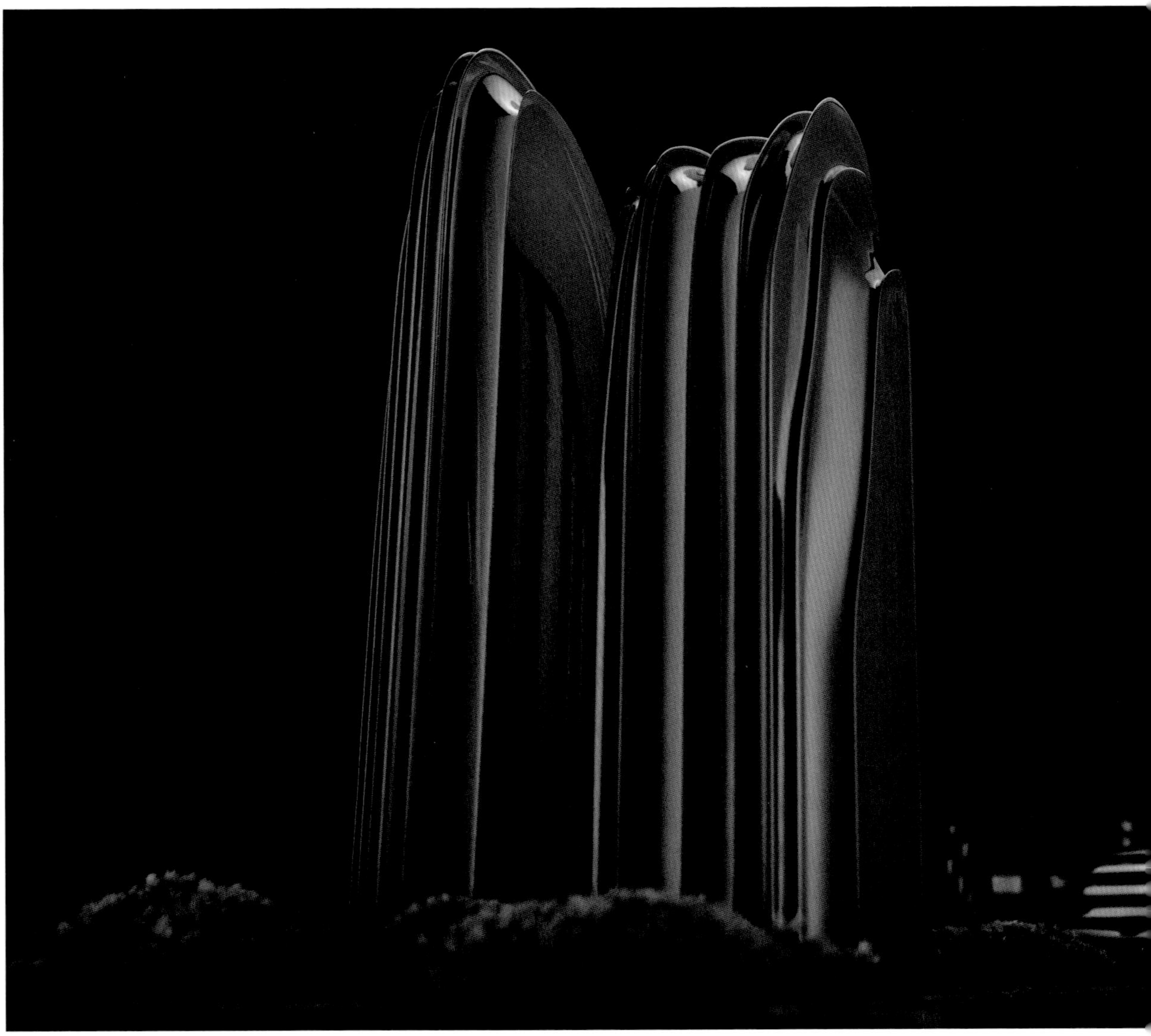

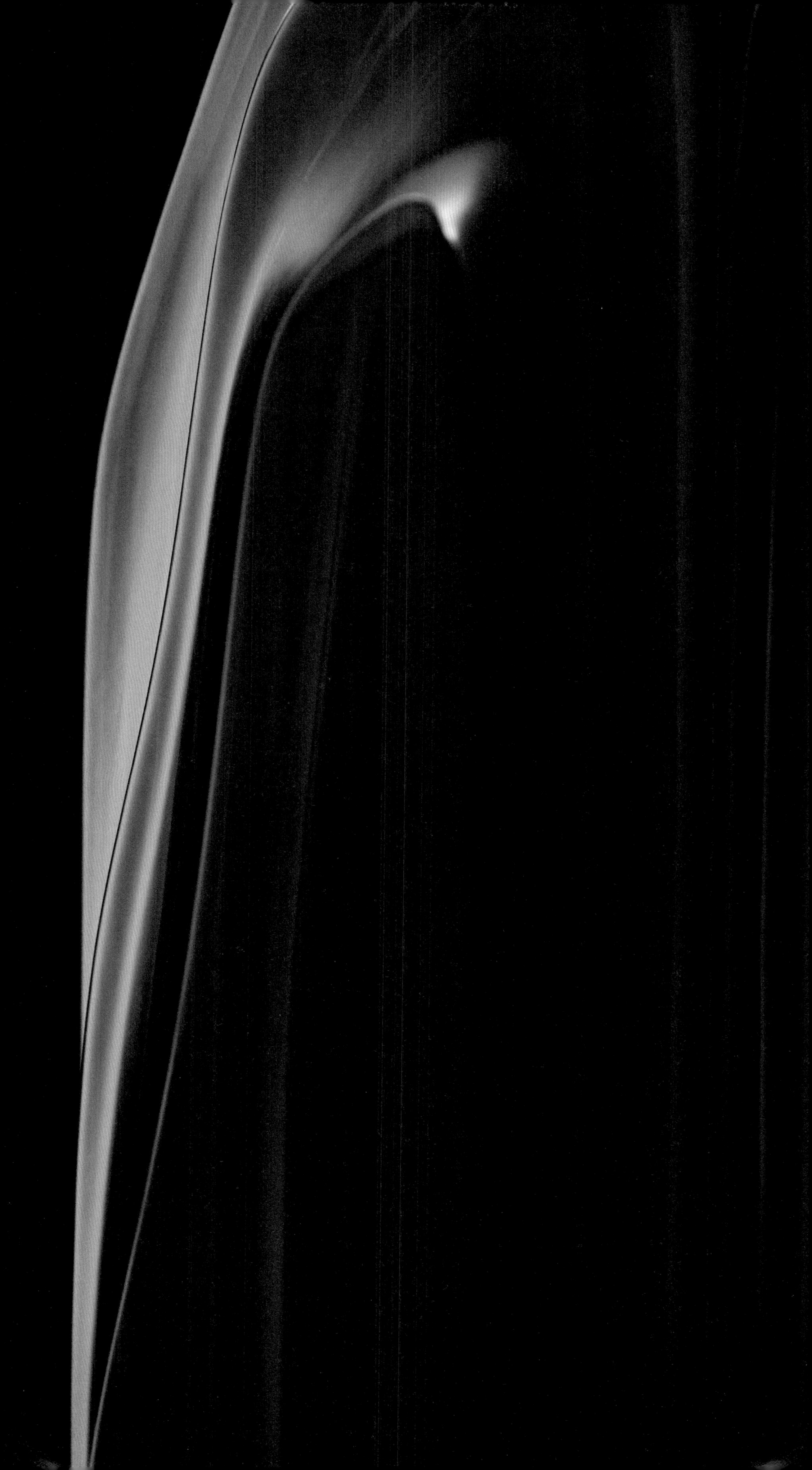

Pingtan Art Museum

Pingtan, China

2011–2017, Under Construction

This natural museum and man-made island hints at its eventual return to the sea.
A pier connects island and mainland, city and nature, past and future.
The radiating ripples of the island's outer shell are infused with sand, stone,
fossils and shells–moments of prehistory frozen in amber.
Within the island's trio of gently rising hills,
primeval caverns will house the largest private art collection in Asia,
contrasting the evolution of human culture with the glacial pace of geological time.

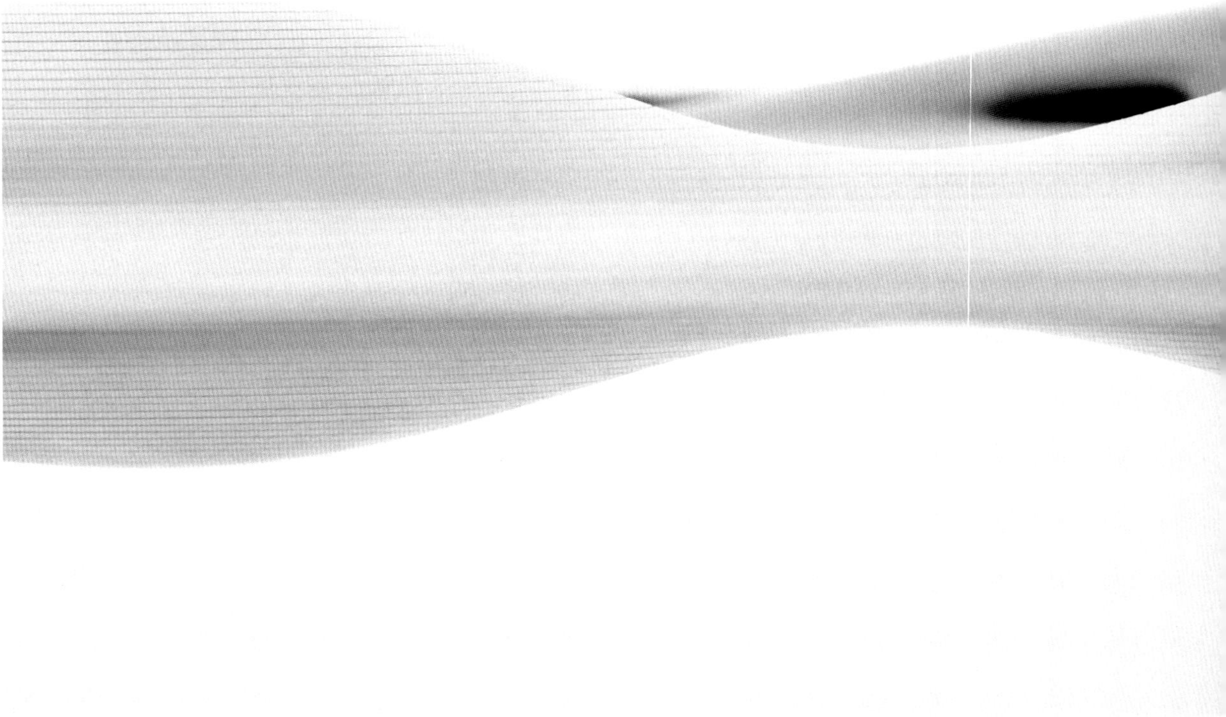

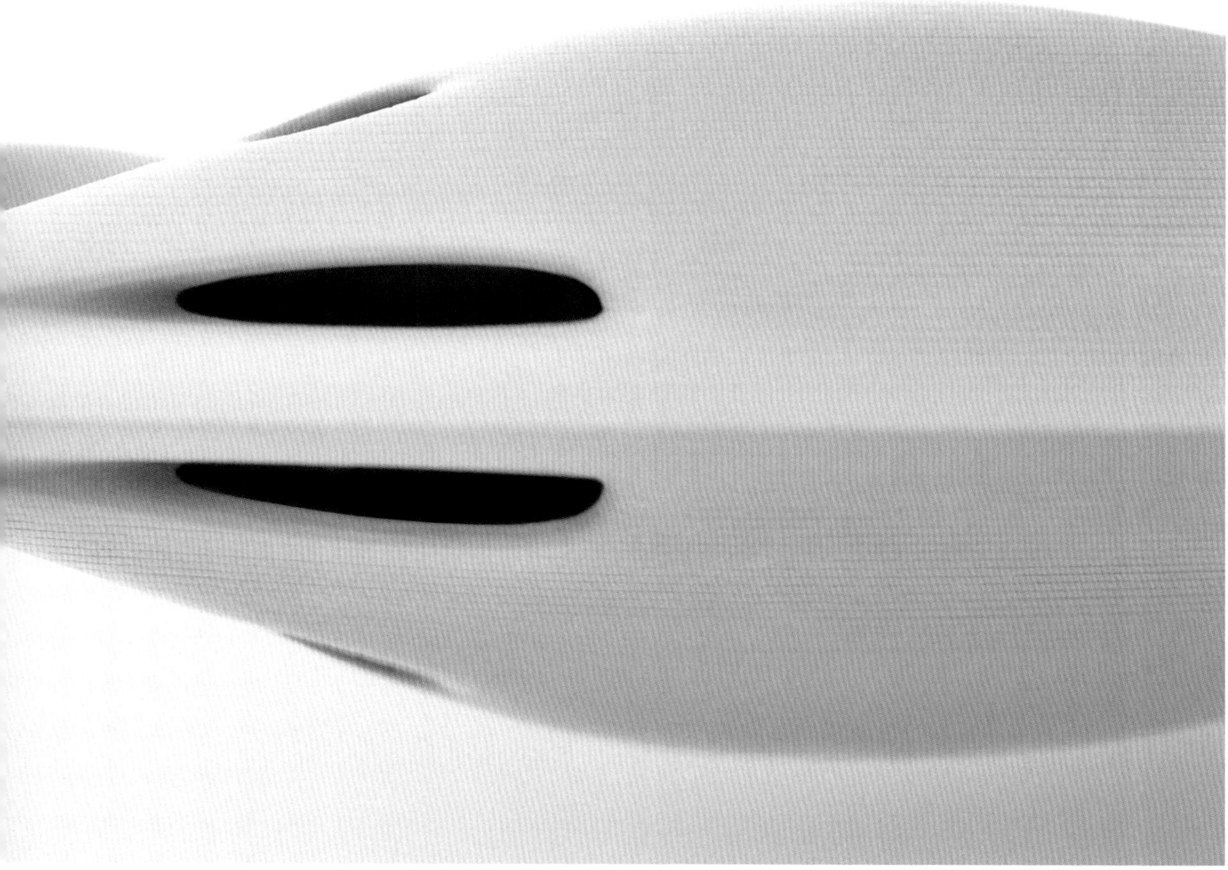

Ordos Museum

Ordos, China

2005–2011

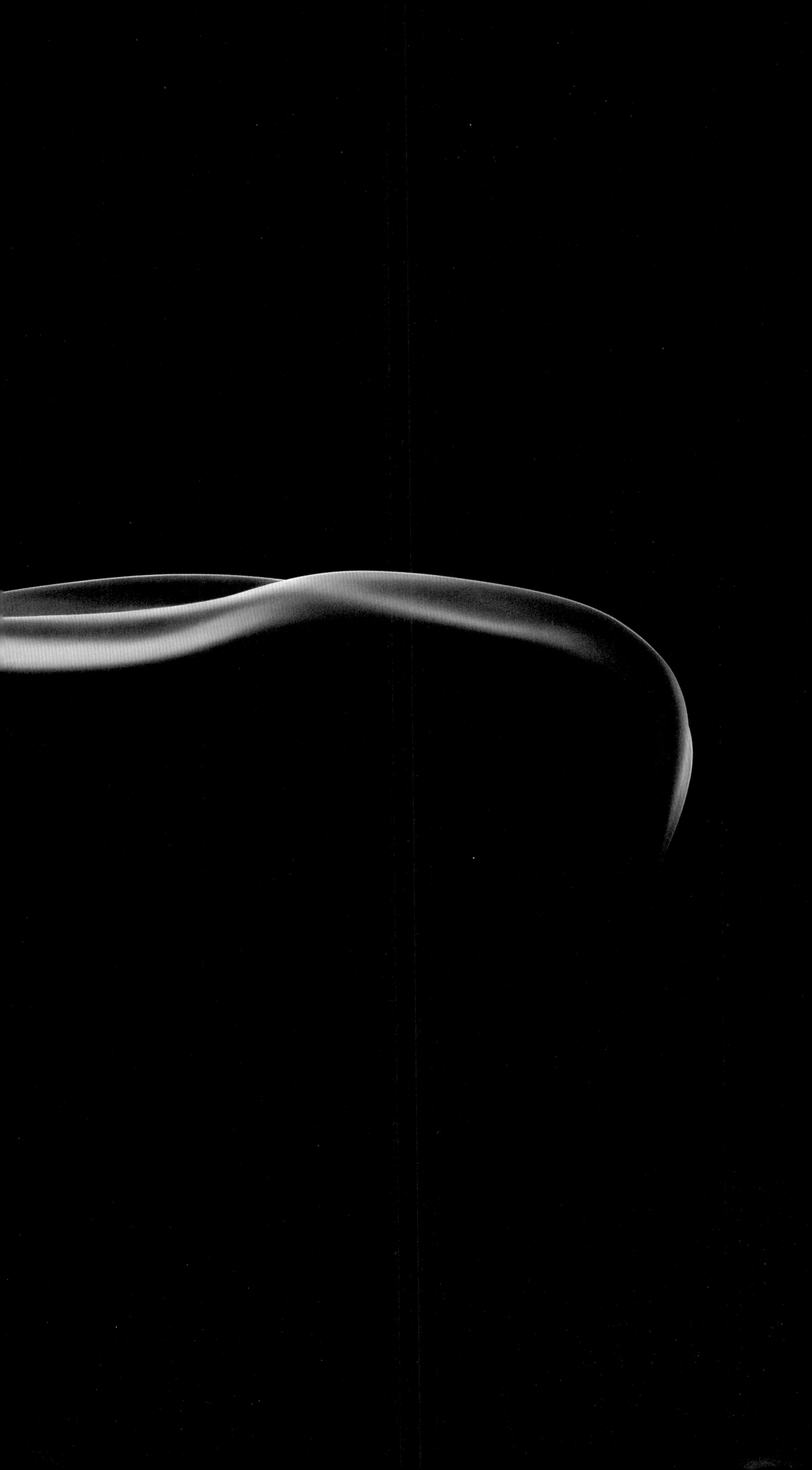

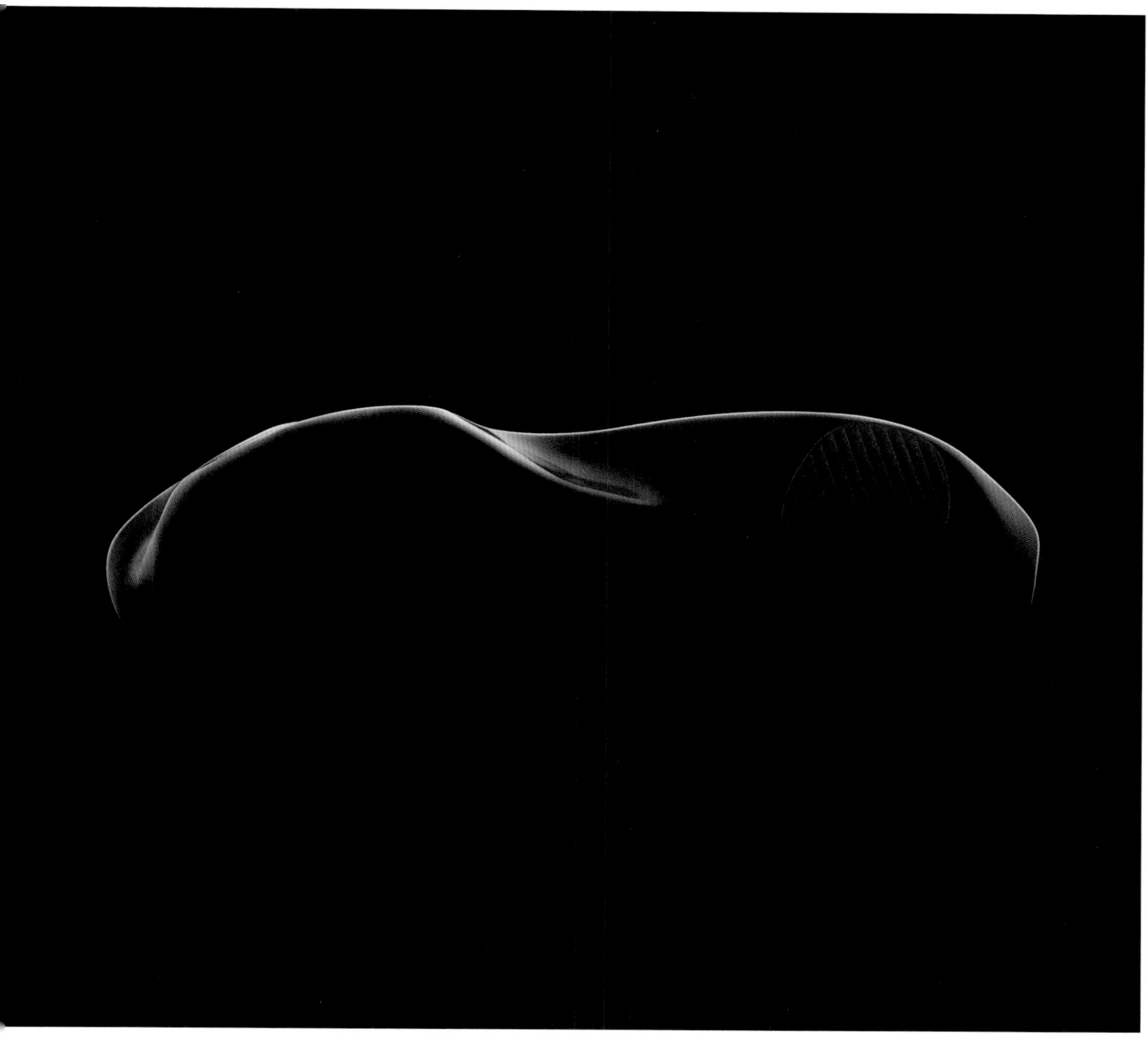

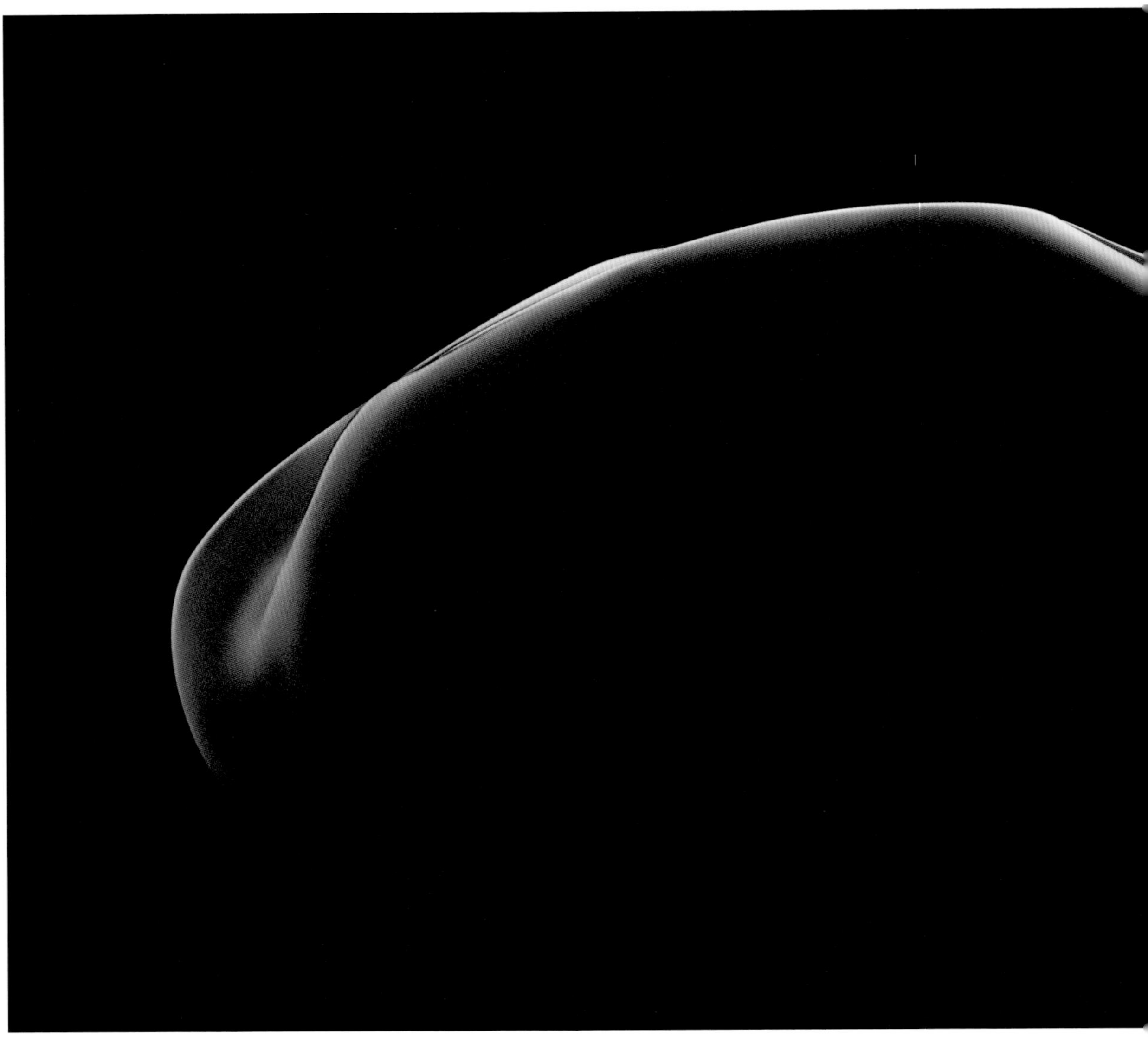

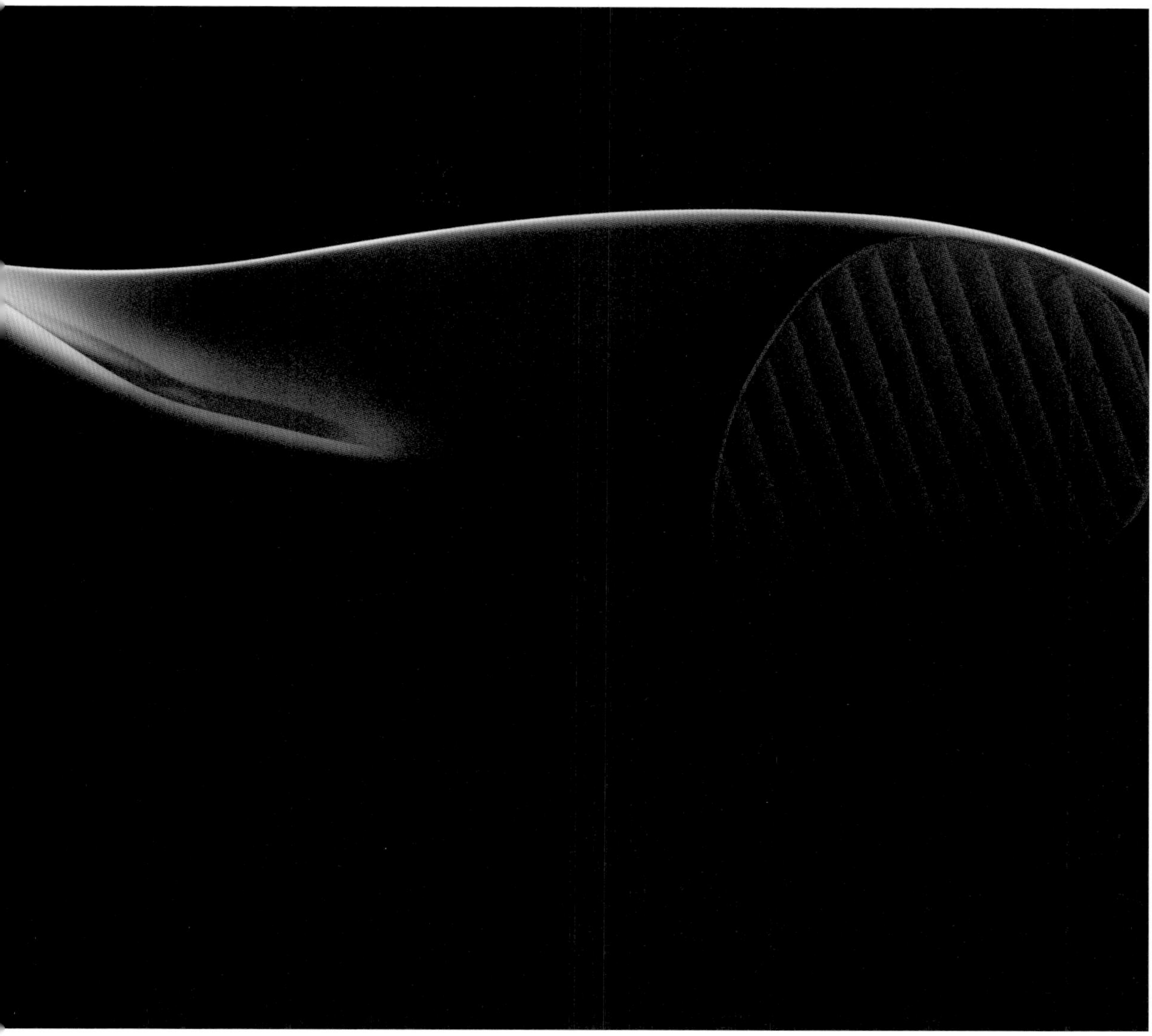

Deep in the Gobi Desert lies a fallen airship of antiquity, or an imposing giant among stones, silently slumbering. This abstract shell isolates interior and exterior. Its undulating, unyielding exterior hints at the Gobi Desert of the past, while challenging the banality of urban structures of the present. The interior provides a refuge from the complexities of city life with its natural grotto-like curves and suspended walkways linking high cliff faces.

China Wood Sculpture Museum

Harbin, China

2009–2013

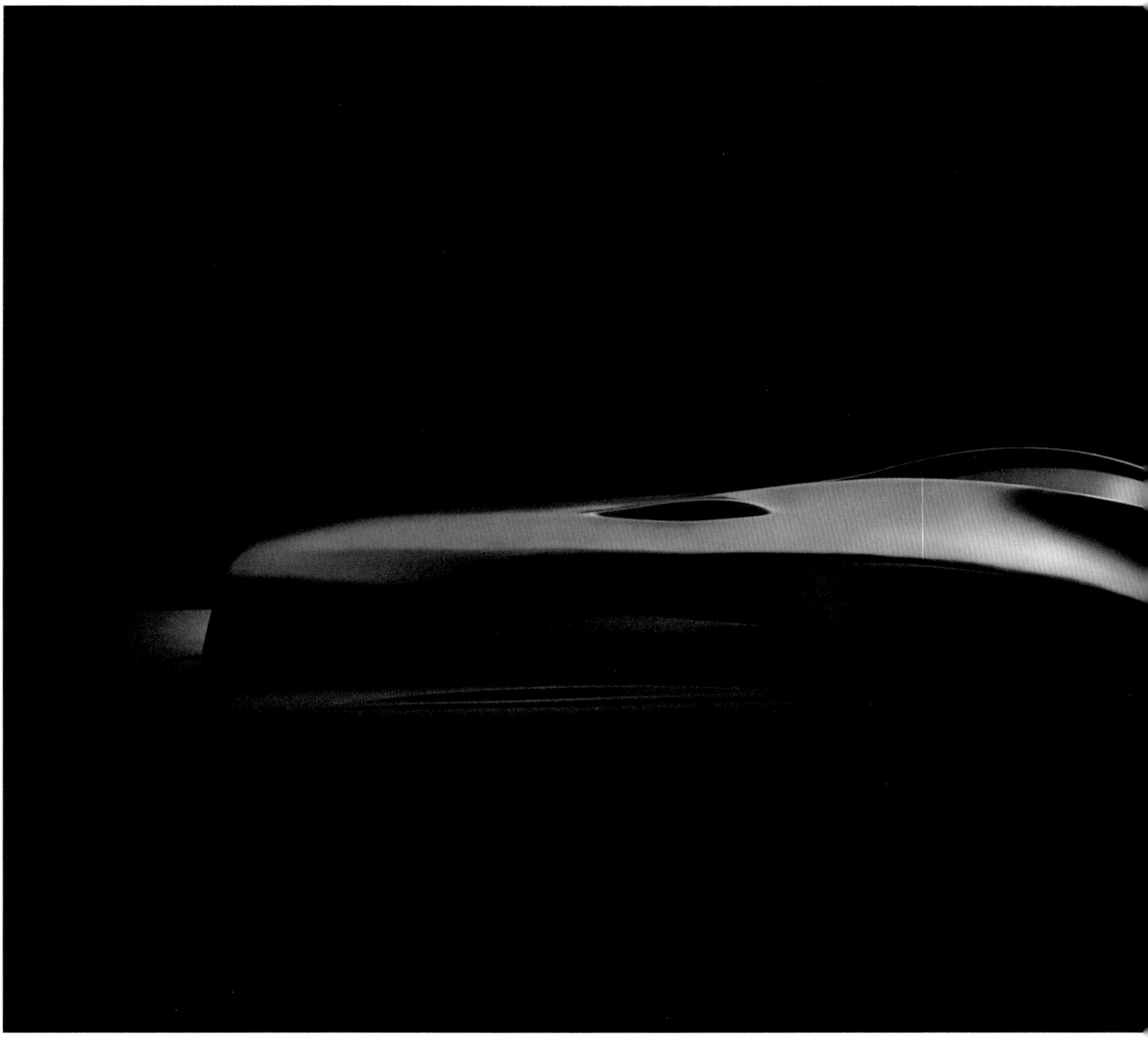

This is a memory of urban alienation, a frozen moment from a future time.
A hybrid of science (fiction) and the (super) natural,
it forms a stark contrast with the residential machines produced by breakneck urbanization.
Its chaotic and abstract form enacts a dislocation in time.

Absolute Towers

Mississauga, Canada

2006–2012

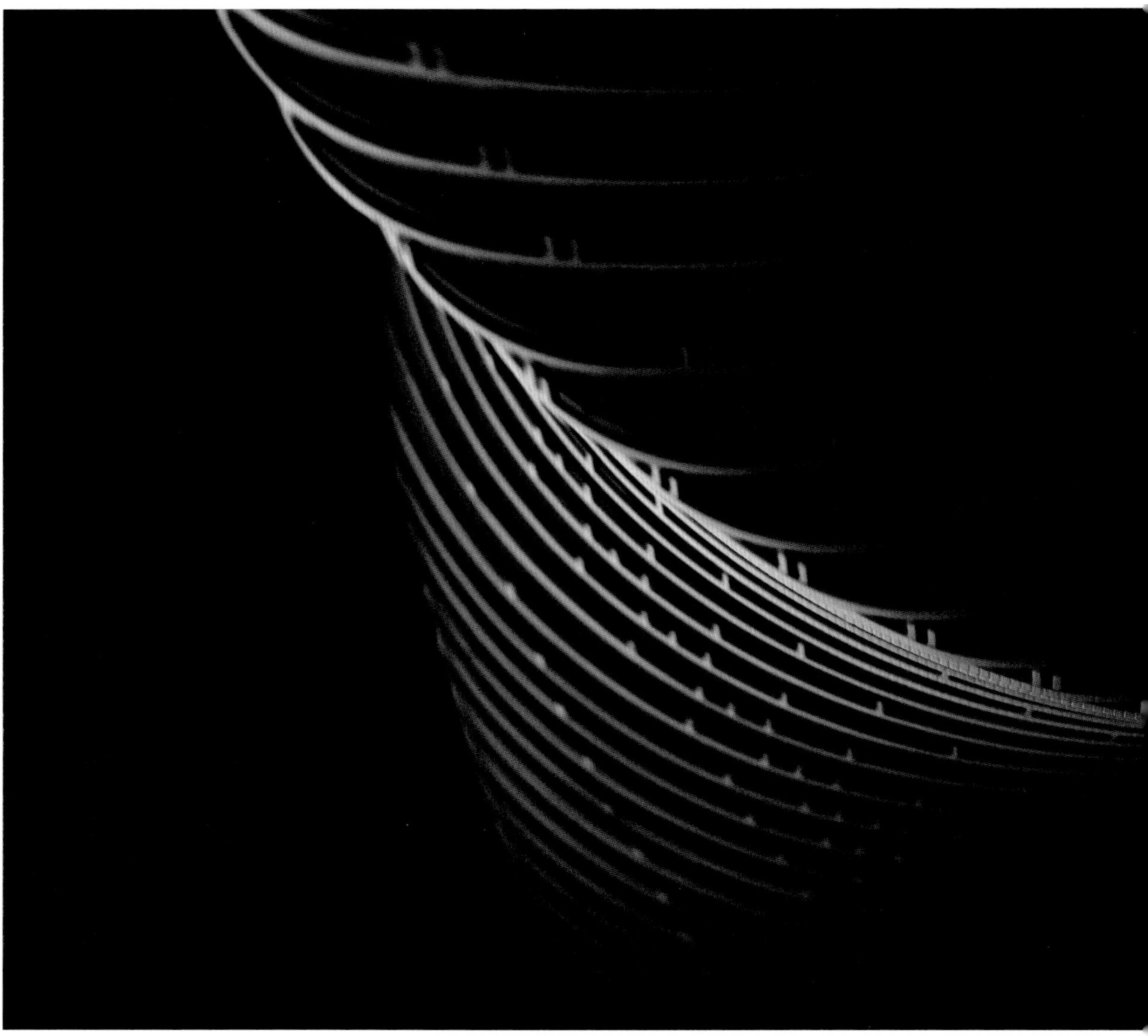

These organic structures twist and stretch up to the sky in time with the cycles of breath.
360-degree views bring residents into contact with sunlight and rain,
the rhythms of nature, and the pulse of the city.
The sinuous anthropomorphic curves of these residences have inspired local the Canadians to nickname them the "Marilyn Monroe Towers"

Fake Hills

Beihai, China

2010–2016

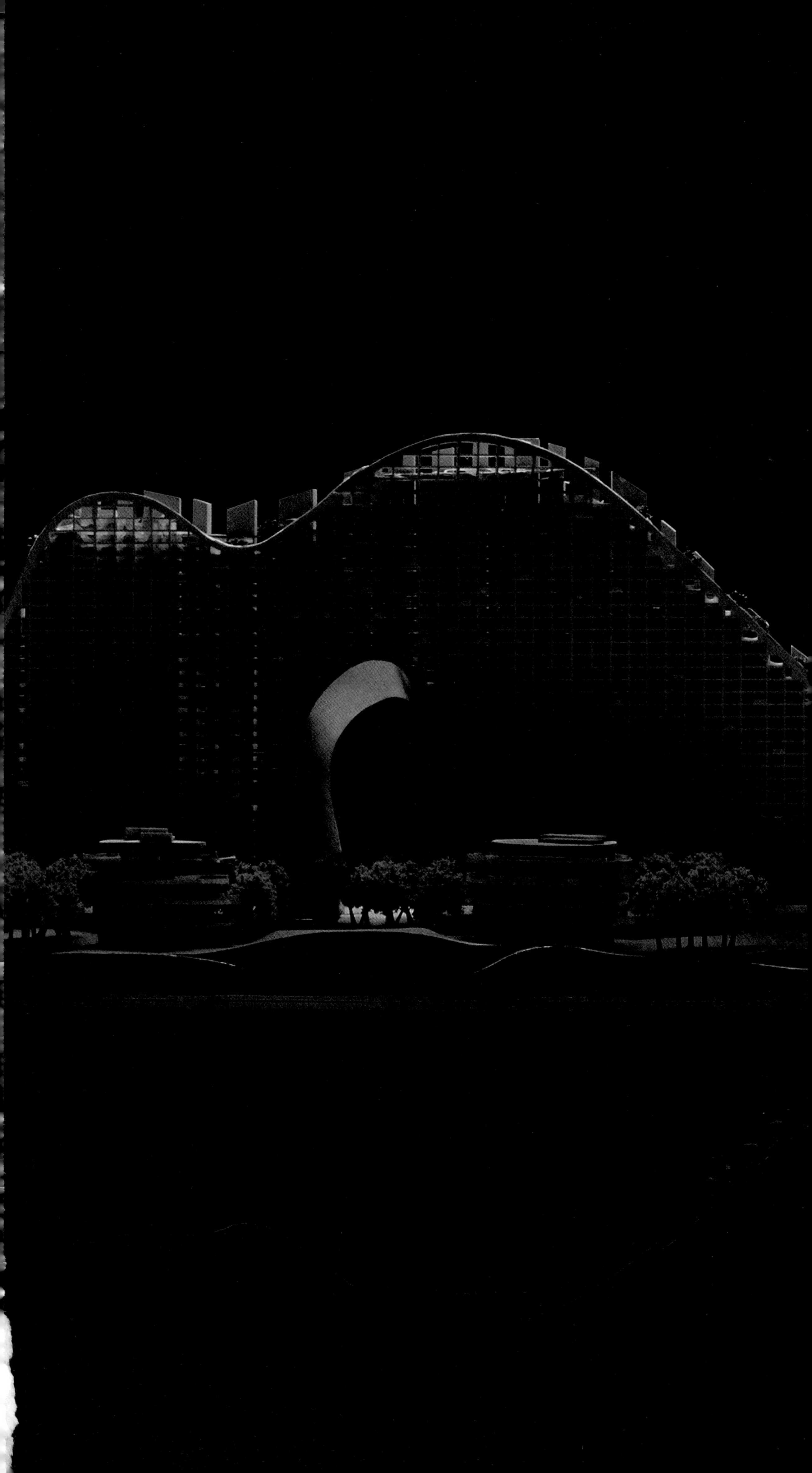

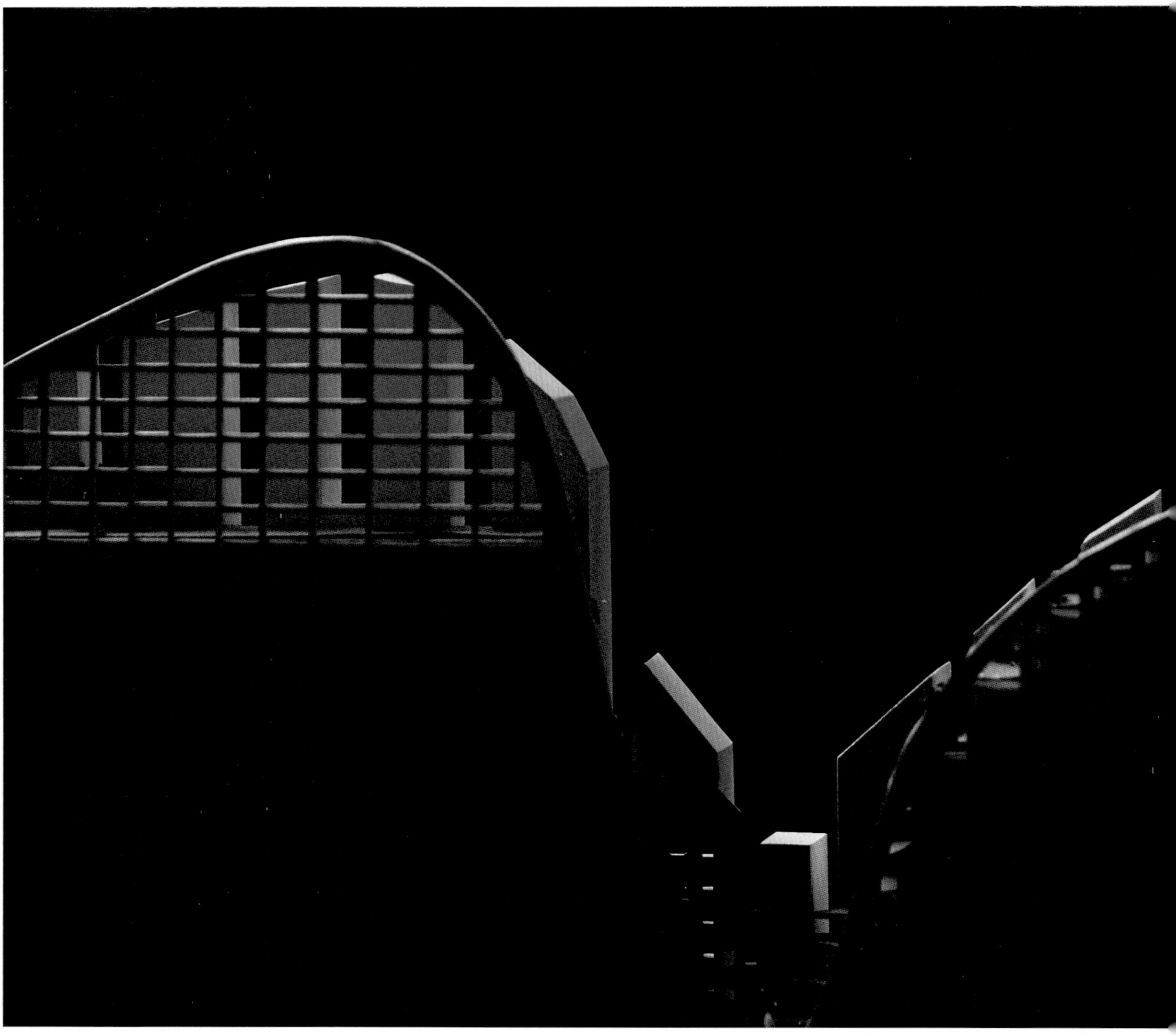

While gazing at the sea, I found myself thinking of hills...
Fake Hill was sketched with a few simple strokes of a pen.
It is not a direct representation of a series of hills,
nor is it a mathematically generated abstraction.
It is an emotional act; its origin lies in affection. It is a simple, free-flowing response
to the urban landscape, enabling a dialogue between the city and the sea.

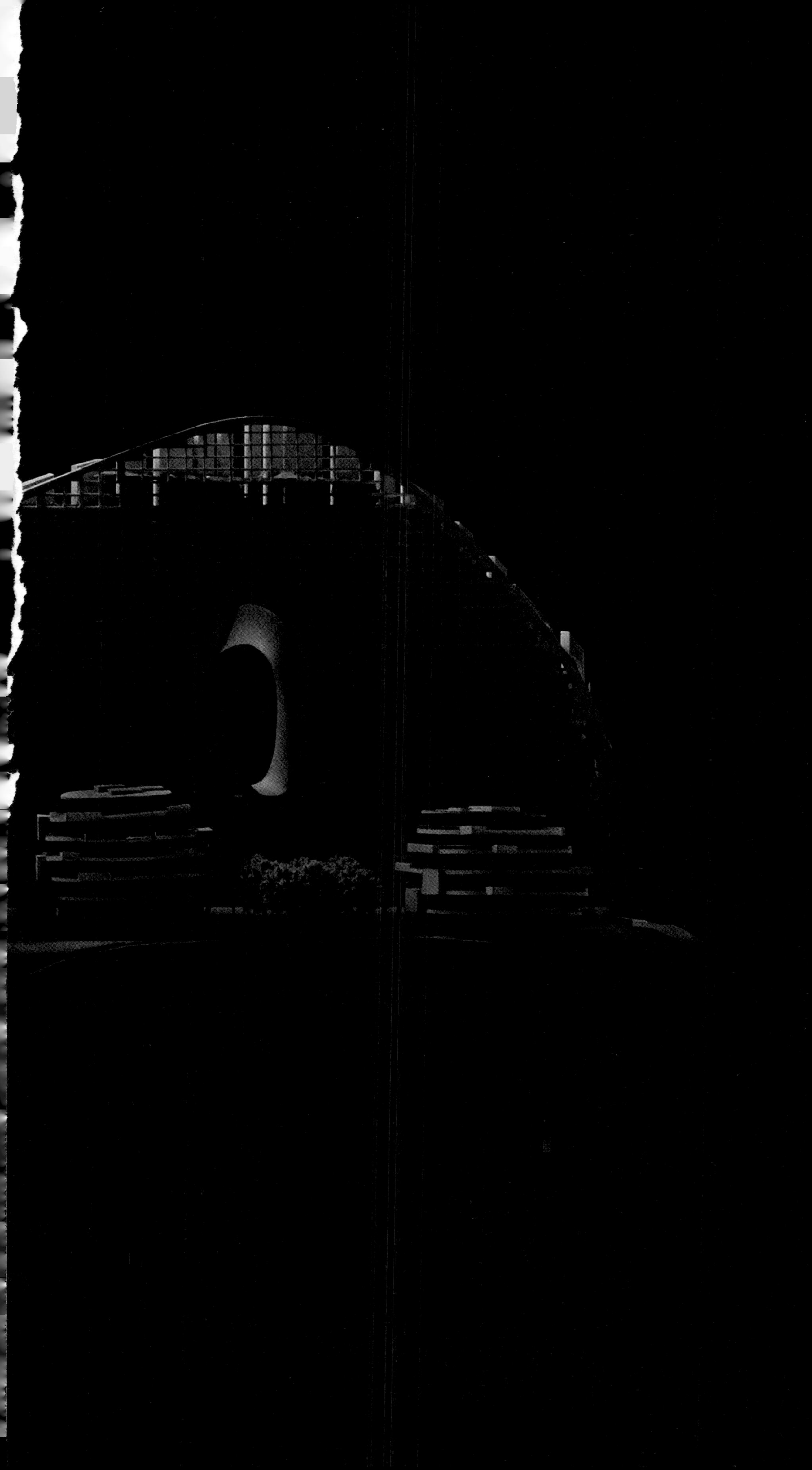

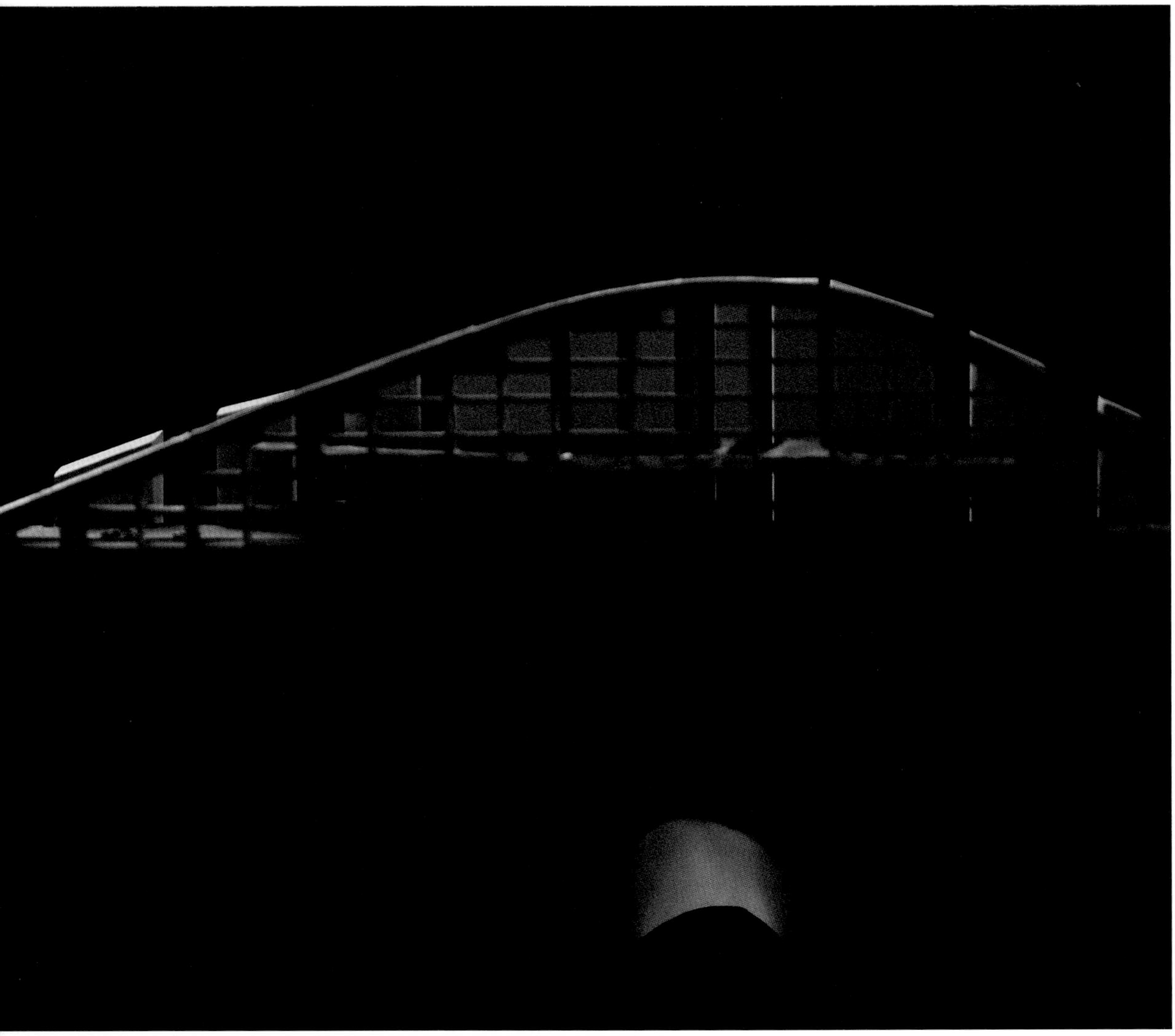

Harbin Culture Center

Harbin, China

2010–2014

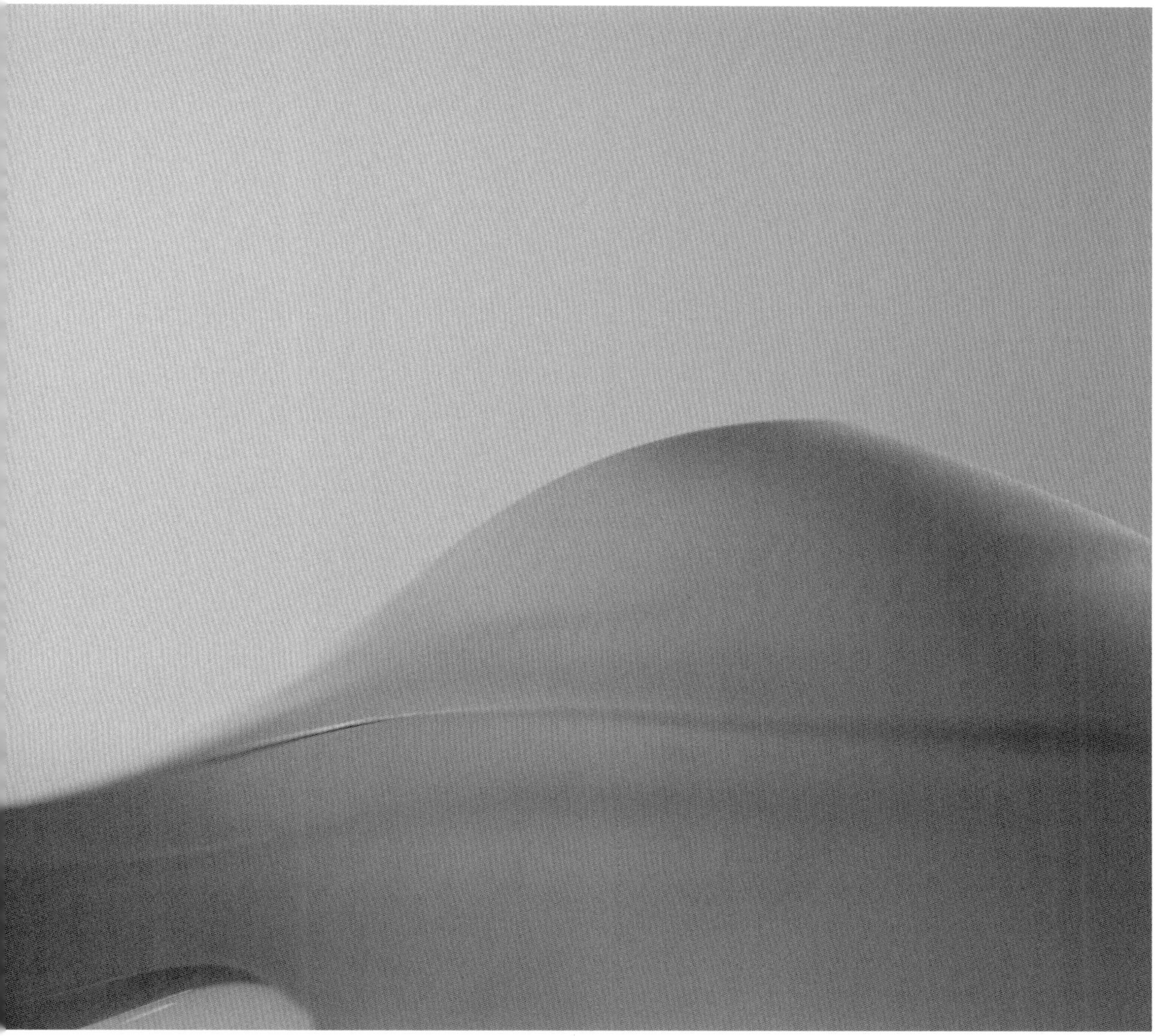

Undulating mountain curves, artificial wetlands, lakes, bridges,
and winding "mountain roads" beautifully integrate this cultural center into its environment.
The rear curtain of the theater rises to reveal a panorama of exterior scenery,
forming a living backdrop to the performance on stage.

Huangshan Mountain Village

Huangshan, China

2009–2015

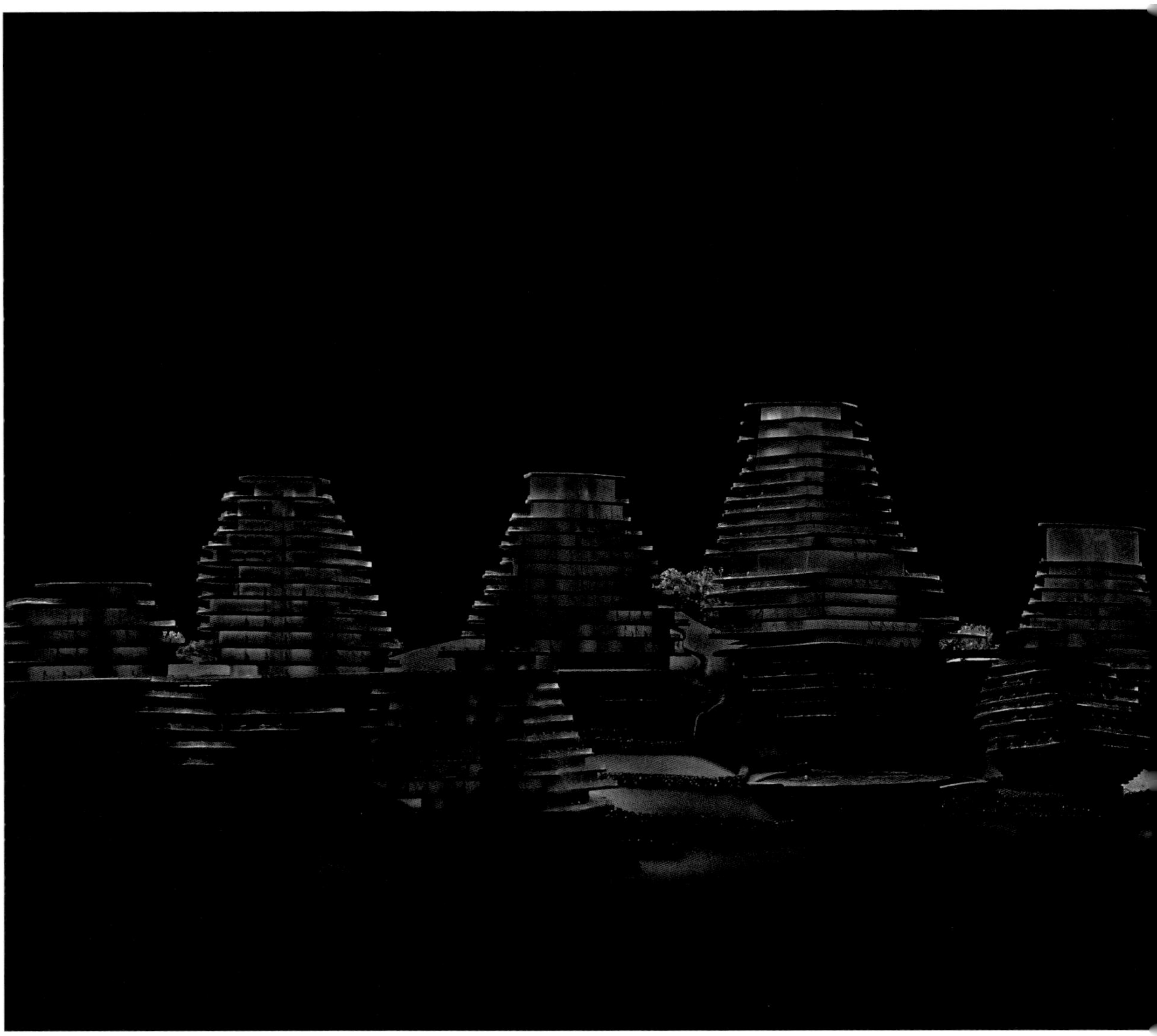

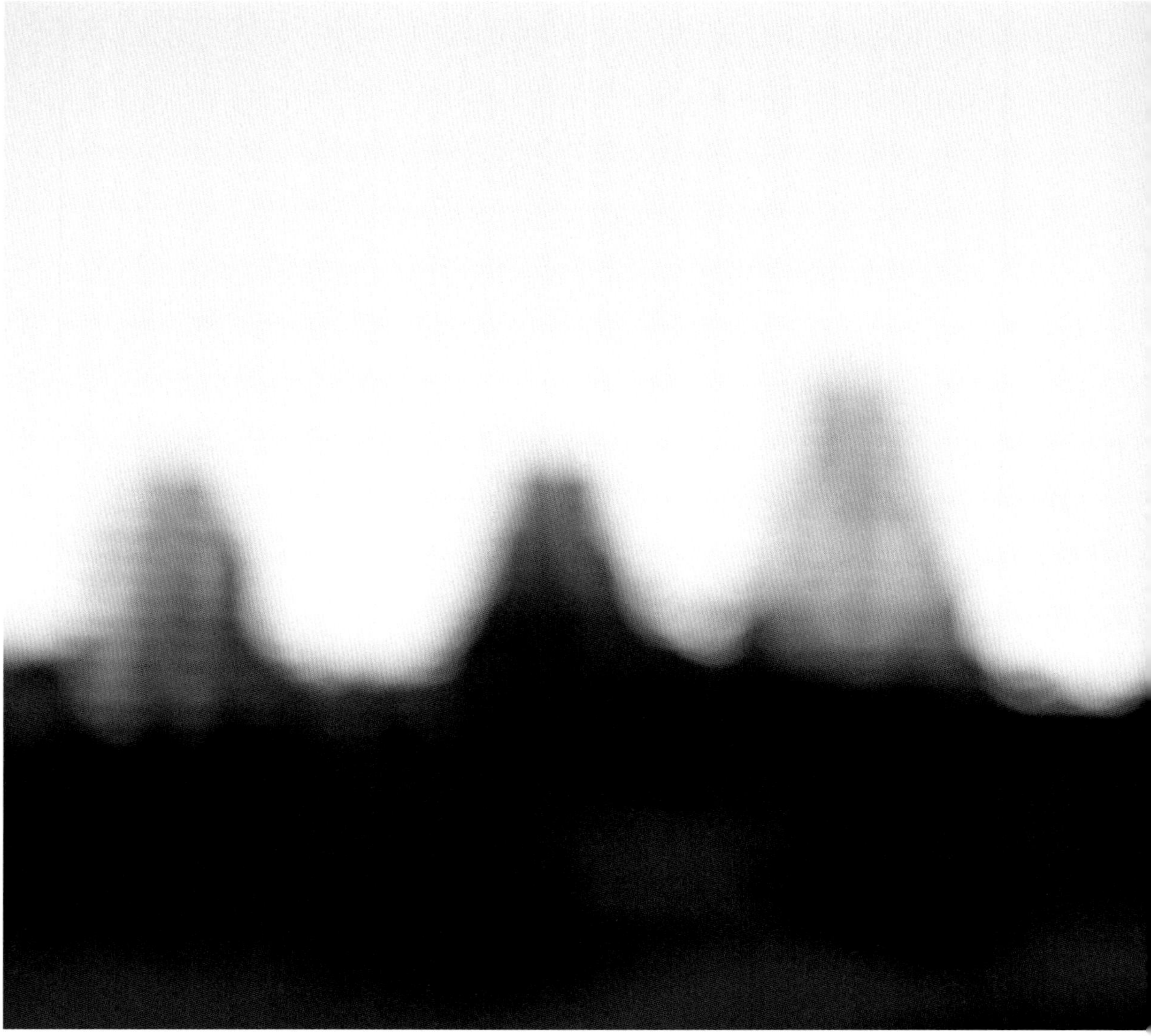

Rippling terraces follow the topography of the mountain, like rice fields of old.
Light and shadow dance on water within the harmonious interplay of mountain and lake.
In this landscape of lake and ridge, architecture becomes nature,
and nature dissolves into architecture.

Fish Tank

2004

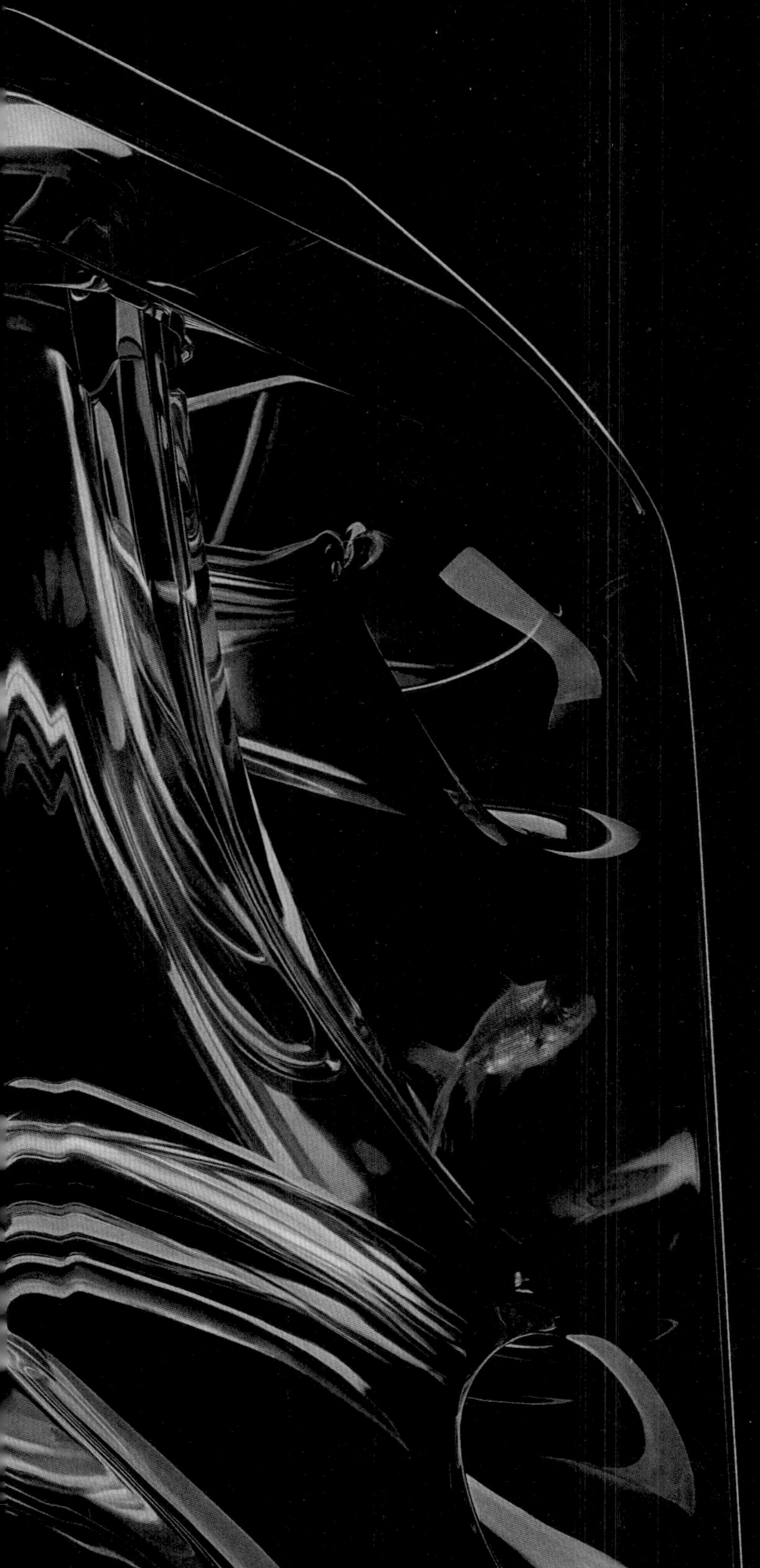

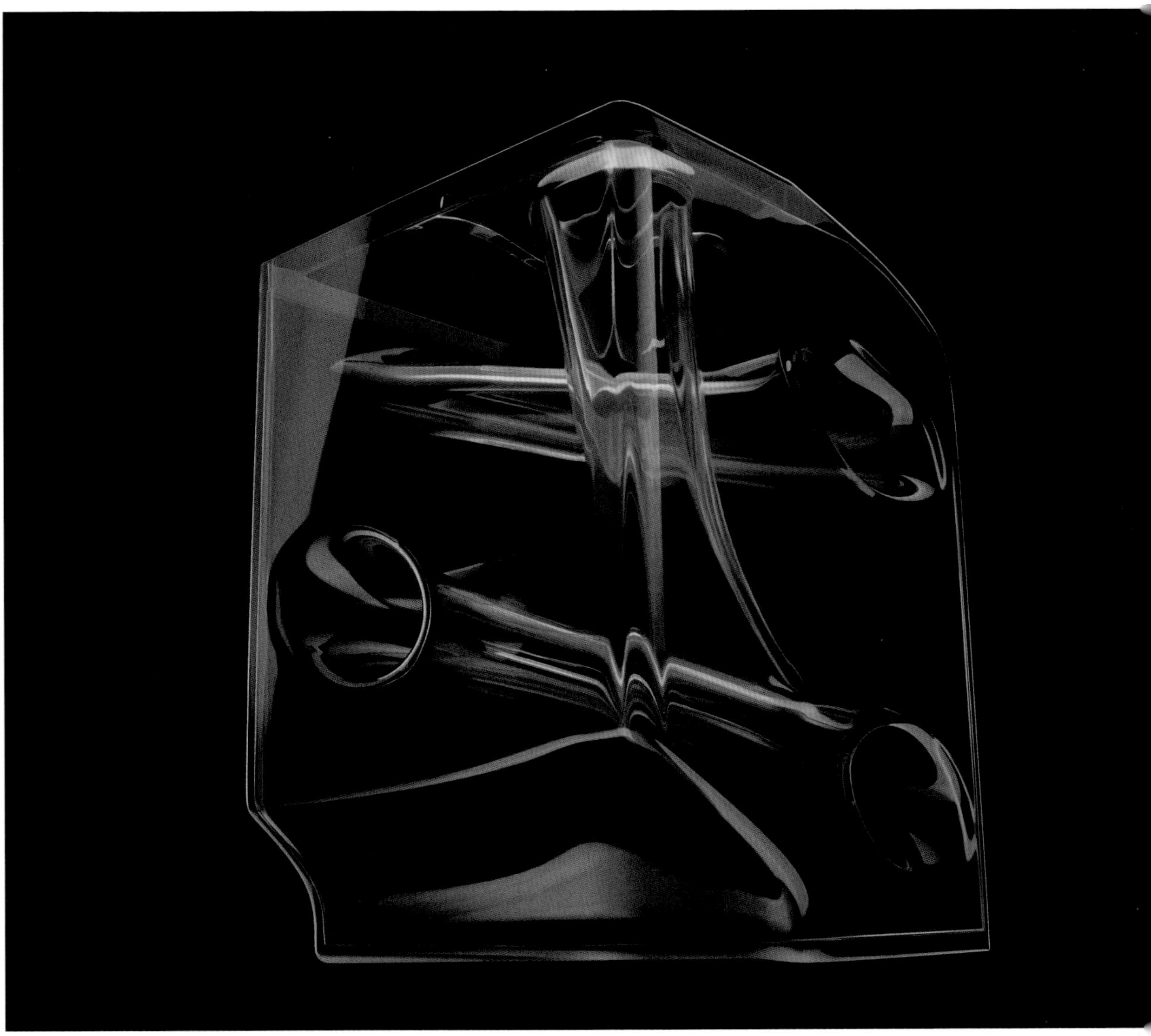

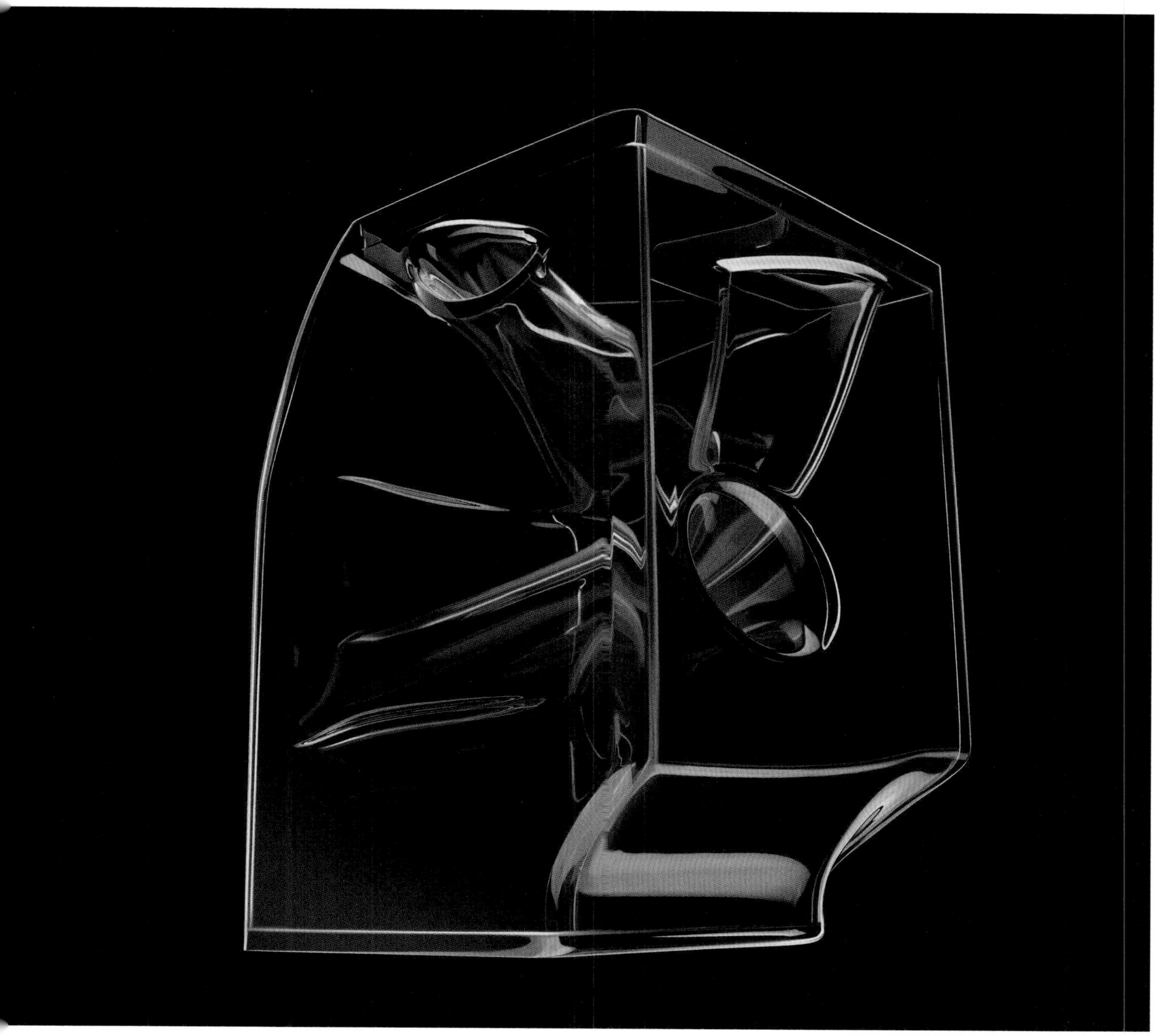

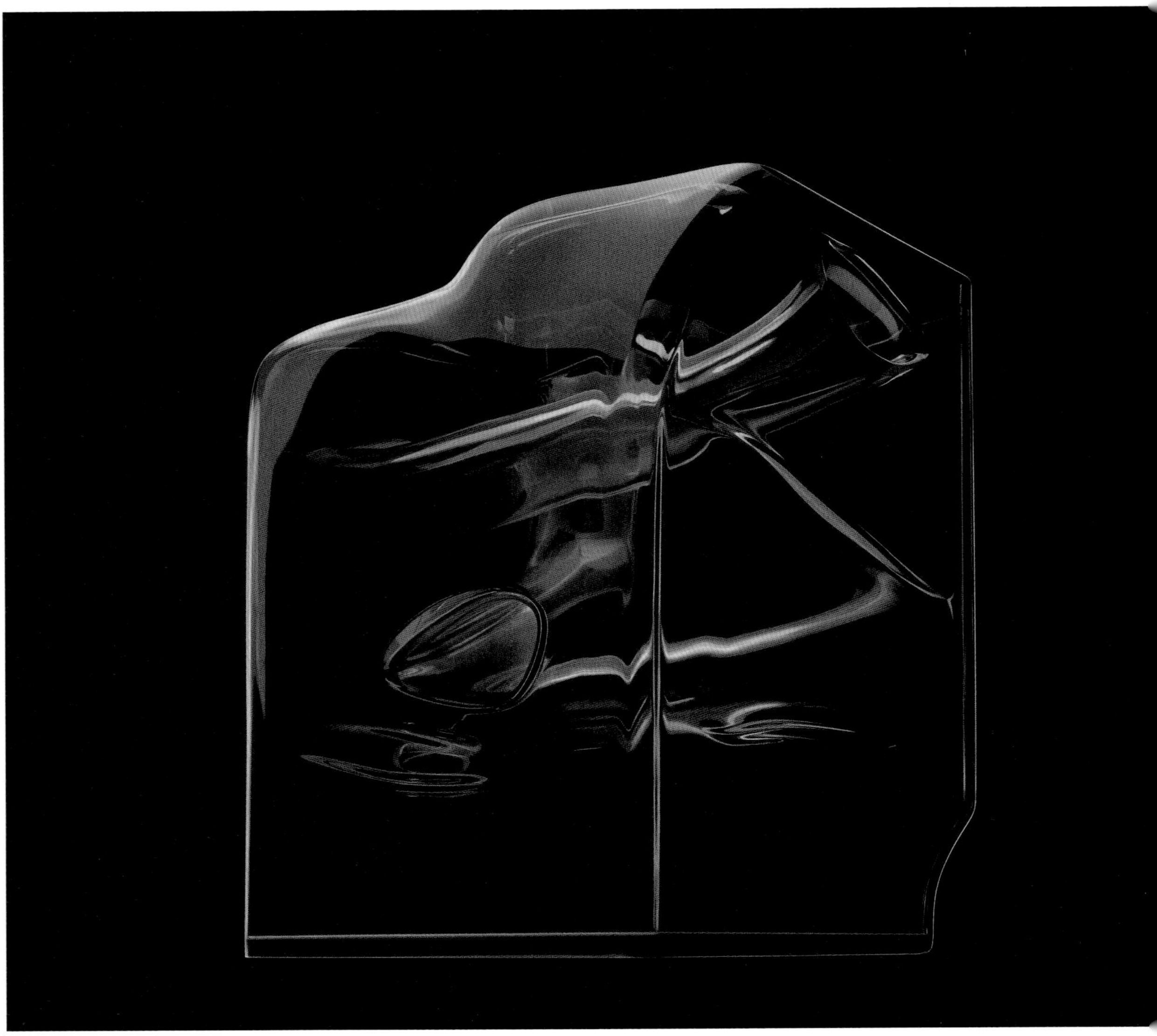

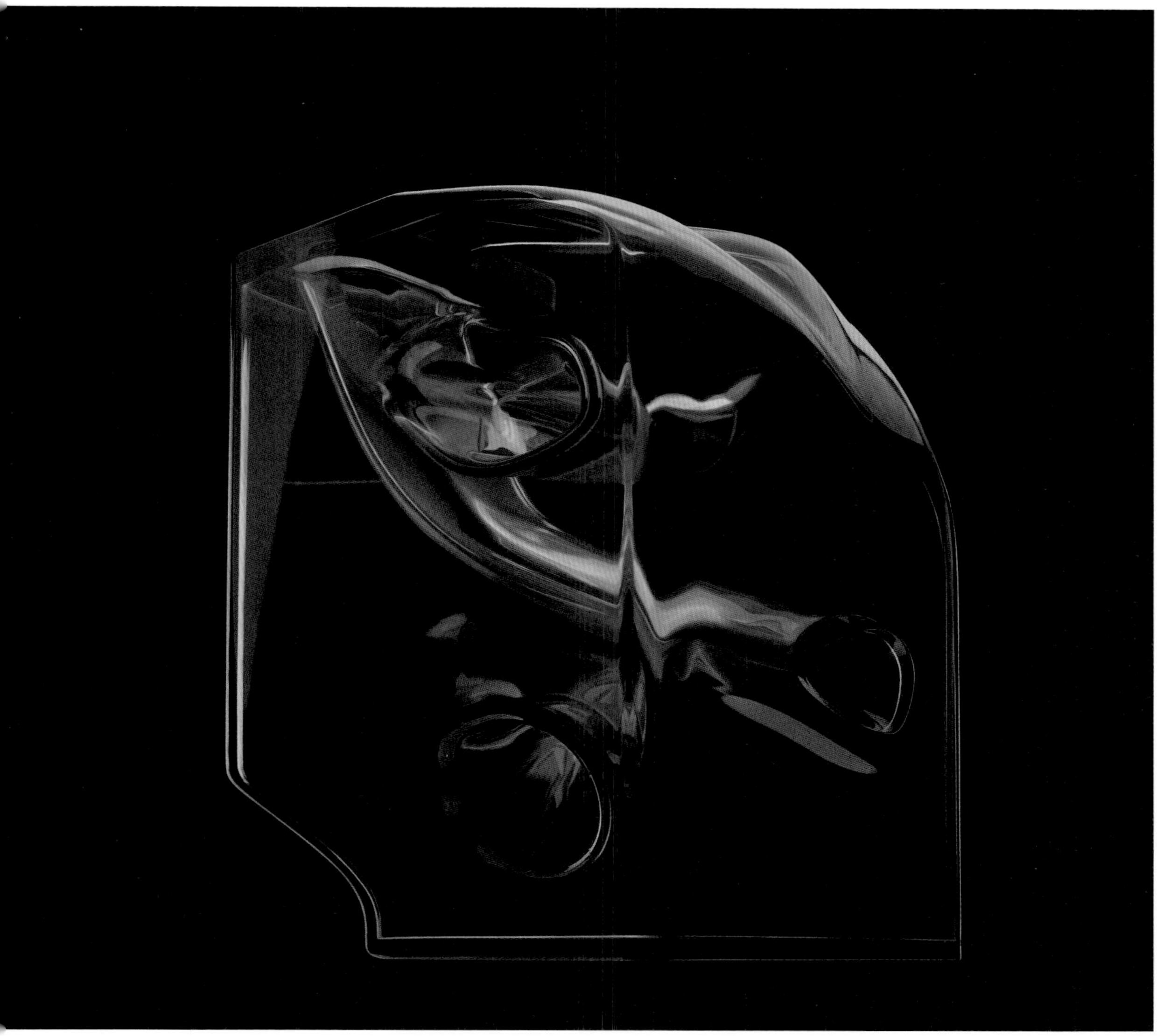

We are searching
For a place where fish might live in the city
The state of man and fish
Must be overturned
Fish are the subject
Space begins to fracture
The square box has thawed
The inferior cube collapses
The machine age has ended
Surfaces
Continue to melt

Interior and exterior blur and connect
The outer surface of the pipe,
the inner surface of the water
Fish
On more outer surfaces
In more complex spaces
Play
The saturation point expands ever outward
Air and water are displaced
Concepts of interior and exterior weaken
Like cyberspace

More free

More hopeful

The boundaries that demarcate

our rights have softened

The square box becomes the enemy

Not in opposition to mainstream culture

The people are the wardens of mainstream ideals

They need more attention

More autonomy

Non-linear Utopia

The Architectural Practice of Ma Yansong

Li Xiangning

A Dialogue with Nature

On That Which Is Essential to the Future of Urban Civilization

Wang Mingxian

Non-linear Utopia

The Architectural Practice of Ma Yansong

Li Xiangning

Against a backdrop of complex social and cultural realities, contemporary Chinese architects adopt a variety of survival strategies and norms of practice. Each practice establishes its own unique position within the complicated networks of architectural autonomy/social reality, global/local, and political/formal. This framework ought to be taken into account when attempting to interpret the work of Ma Yansong.

Ma is one of the most internationally influential and distinctive personalities within contemporary Chinese architecture. From his relatively early works Fish Tank, Ink Ice, and Hutong Bubble, up to his recent large-scale works, like Absolute Towers, Ordos Museum, and the Lucas Museum of Narrative Art in Chicago (for which Ma won the competition against international offices such as Zaha Hadid, OMA and UNStudio), we can see his clear and sustained strategy.

Firstly, in terms of architectural language, Ma explores the possibilities of a non-linear formal language, which gives his works an instantly recognizable character. His sustained practice has gradually developed into a strategy in which he integrates this formal language into the unique challenges and issues of Chinese urbanization. Reviewing contemporary Chinese architecture, the overwhelming influx of international architectural consultants has turned many design practices into a revolving door of architectural dependency, referencing Dutch, Spanish, and Japanese styles in a clear and sustained exploration of language. Pragmatic strategies have led architects to quickly modify their practice when faced with different clients or objective requirements. Within this environment, Chinese architects have found it difficult to persist in a formal language that bears a unique and immediately recognizable style. Perhaps it's the fact that Ma has managed to establish and sustain a distinct style that has allowed him to become the Chinese architect most well known internationally.

Secondly, in the age of contemporary media, Ma excels at defining a clear media strategy. Contemporary architectural culture is a synthetic system of production. The work itself is just one link within a system of socio-economics, politics, design, construction, and dissemination. Parallel to the conceptual developments within contemporary art, architecture is not merely an unchanging collection of individual work, but the initial link within a chain of processes for the production and dissemination of images. Apart from the works themselves, the architect's philosophy and writings, his role as a theorist and transmitter of culture, as well as his advocacy for contemporary architecture are all tremendously valuable. Ma's projects, including publications, exhibitions, forums, critiques, and even an international travel scholarship, prove that his abilities and worldview are international in scope.

Over the course of Ma's career, starting from when he began participating in dozens of competitions after his return to China, to his present focus on a small number of large-scale buildings, he has never abandoned the theoretical critique and utopianism central to his works. Floating Island, Beijing 2050, Shanghai Modern Art Park (S-MAP), and other conceptual designs all have the character of urban manifestos, echoing the spirit of designs by 1960s offices like Superstudio and Archizoom. Since the decline of the US economy, a number of journals of architectural theory closed shop as editors and theorists have taken positions as tenured professors in well-respected universities. Apart from those working in parametrically generated design, there is a dearth of theoretical architects in the US who can surpass the likes of Peter Eisenman and Steven Holl. It is as if critical energy has run dry in the West. China now has the opportunity to contribute its unique critical stance to the discourse. From the very beginning Ma's works of architecture and urban design have provided much-needed critical energy to the discipline.

In recent years, Ma's thinking and non-linear practice have gradually incorporated the concept of the Shanshui City. In traditional Shanshui, the architect uses construction as a means to enter into and alter the natural landscape, overturning the subject/object relationships in nature. With regard to the connections between building, dwelling, and critical thought indicated by Heidegger, constructing a house becomes a material and mental activity that manifests subjective existence.

Traditional Chinese scholars saw the construction of gardens as a means of establishing a connection with nature. Landscape gardening was an active means of reconstructing the natural environment for which they longed. Intellectuals who were frustrated with their political careers dreamt of the freedom of a life in the wilderness, away from the political center. But due to their lingering Confucian aspirations and the allure of political power, they could never truly turn their backs on urban life. Therefore, they simulated nature within their urban residences as a kind of spiritual compensation. Shanshui is an image of the natural world created within the subconscious to act as consolation and compensation for the struggles of political life.

Today, the possibilities contained within modern construction technologies have overturned our concept of the relationship between humankind and Shanshui. Traditional literati landscape architecture, for the most part, attempted to simulate the vast scenery of mountains and waters on a micro-scale. Ma's works use high-rise architecture and even entire cities to create a real Shanshui; an actual landscape in which people live and work. It is the same vision active in the creation of a garden, simply magnified several hundred, thousand, or even ten thousand times. The power of the soaring Chinese economy combined with the possibilities of new construction technologies enable today's architects to do more than just place square buildings in the middle of natural landscapes. Nor are they limited to the narcissistic micro-landscapes of private gardens and bonsai. Digital design technology unlocks the power of the imagination, allowing architecture and the city itself to become Shanshui. The formal contrast in traditional gardens between the geometry of architecture and the organic forms of the environment, however minimal it may be, has finally disappeared. Architecture can be stacked and staggered to form lofty volumes reminiscent of mountain ranges, or it can lie in close proximity to the earth, more like rolling hills.

Just as traditional gardens were used by academics as a spiritual buffer against the stresses and disappointments of competitive political life, so perhaps Shanshui Cities might be able to ameliorate the urban nightmare faced by contemporary Chinese architects. Their latent longing for Shanshui is in part a reaction to fears of oppressive smog, unbearable congestion, and food safety scandals. Contemporary artists have explored complicated reactions to the conditions of modern urban life, taking into account both the alienation and anxiety of urban existence, as well as the longing for nature and nostalgia for a simpler life. Likewise architects do not simply concentrate on the distress, anxiety, and doubt of modern life. Instead, they move one step further, and offer a new prospect for the future. They enlist the tools made available by the booming economy and advancing technology to combat the dystopia of our deepest fears. The resulting marriage of urban ambition and traditional Chinese philosophy yields directions that are actually very similar to Le Corbusier's Ville Radieuse, Frank Lloyd Wright's Broadacre City, the cities of the Japanese Metabolism Movement, and Yona Friedman's Spatial City. They all look to the cities of our predecessors as models through which to criticize and correct the various defects of our contemporary cities. For all of them, technology is the means to realize a set of ideals with the potential to change the course of future urbanization, in both theory and practice.

When I curated the 2013 Shenzhen and Hong Kong Bi-City Biennale of Urbanism/Architecture, the exhibition featured a gigantic model of Ma's Nanjing Zendai Himalayas Center in which he imagines the city as an enormous bonsai landscape. This vast space dedicated to vegetation, bodies of water, and curling mist attracted the attention of many visitors. In lieu of the "architect-as-savior" narrative, I am more inclined to regard this experiment as one of many differing responses to the circumstances of contemporary Chinese society. Regardless of whether these responses come in the form of a large-scale fabricated utopian city or a more activist rural construction movement, they all confront the same fears and anxieties—anxieties rooted in the societal realities of contemporary China and the estrangement between contemporary humanity, environment, and memory. In this sense, I tend to see a common movement of resistance within this wide variety of architectural solutions. Whether a specific solution advocates grassroots social activism or human-made environments on the massive scale of Ma's Shanshui Cities, both are critical tools that indicate dissatisfaction with existing models of urban life and construction. When regarding Ma's works, I find I have a preference for the projects that utilize non-linearity to create a distinctive utopian atmosphere. Within their "mountains" and "water" lies a hidden logic which brings us into contact with the surging pulse of Chinese society, yet transcends the specific problems of the Chinese city. Through Ma's work we become integrated into a universal vision of an urban future suitable for a global age.

Li Xiangning | Professor of History, Theory and Criticism
at Tongji University College of Architecture and Urban Planning

Li Xiangning is a young scholar and critic of contemporary Chinese architecture. He has published widely on contemporary architecture and urbanism in China. He was chief curator of the 2010 Sanya Design Biennale and co-curator of the 2011 Chendu Biennale and the 2011 Shenzhen Biennale.

A Dialogue with Nature

On That Which Is Essential to the Future of Urban Civilization

Wang Mingxian

If we take the publication of the first Chinese architectural studies of the modern era as a starting point, then the study of contemporary architecture in China has existed for over one hundred years. In July 1910, the Commercial Press published Zhang Yingxu's *New Principles of Architecture*, laying the foundation for Chinese modern architecture. From the early twentieth century to the present, Chinese architects have undertaken the important work of importing Western architectural thought and solving a vast number of architectural problems within Chinese society. However, it is also worthwhile to consider whether Chinese architects of the twentieth century produced any ideas that were influential on a global scale. Some scholars have pointed out that the Chinese architectural community lacks global influence of the kind exhibited by Japan's Metabolism Movement of the 1960s. Published by a group of young Japanese architects in 1960, *Metabolism 1960-Proposal for a New Urbanism* explored an entirely new path for urbanism. Alongside their experimental architectural practice, the group developed a large number of futurist-tinged concepts concerning the city. The birth of the Metabolism Movement proved to be an historic moment, and its young protagonists became emblematic figures of the post-World War II Japanese cultural renaissance.

Despite Chinese architecture's lack of global influence, the work of certain younger and mid-career Chinese architects over the past decade is worth noting. Many of them take the relationship between architecture and nature as their point of entry into the issues of contemporary Chinese architecture. Since the advent of the twenty-first century, one direction of research pursued by this new generation of architects has been "returning to nature." In his essay "We Must Return to a Philosophy of Nature," Wang Shu discusses how China and the West hold divergent views on the relationship between humanity and the natural world. In the West, architecture interacts with nature from a position of existential independence; however, in the Chinese cultural tradition, architecture within a natural landscape is merely an object of secondary importance, though one that cannot be neglected. Expressed in another way, in Chinese culture, nature was once far more important than architecture. Architecture acted as a humanmade "natural" object within a larger natural scene. The ancient Chinese devoted great energy to studying and imitating nature, to the point that everyday life was lived in a state of close contact with nature. Living in accord with the "Way of Nature" was the Chinese humanist ideal. Within the aesthetic narrative of contemporary architecture, the planning and design of the Chinese Academy of Art Xiangshan campus rediscovered the traditional Chinese concept of space. The site explores the problem of reconstructing roots within a decaying suburb, acting as a model for the coexistence of Chinese traditions with natural landscapes within our present-day reality. Within its primary goal of "reconstructing a Chinese contemporary local architecture," the traditional Chinese aesthetics concerning the relationship between mountains, water, and architecture have been fashioned anew.

Chinese architects are faced with a number of difficult questions posed by the high-density, fabricated environments that accompany China's massive urbanization project. A new group of young architects, among whom Ma Yansong is a representative figure, are directly confronting these issues. Through a posture of active intervention, their practice floats freely between the interior and the margins of the city. In confronting our modern-day existential plight, they delight in probing the poetics of the city of the future, applying the ideal of the Shanshui City in practice. Seeking out "natural and poetic sentiments within the city," they use Urban Shanshui to structure the city of the future.

In recent years, Ma Yansong's MAD Architects have devoted themselves to incorporating nature into high-density cities. Restoring the relationship between the urban and the natural, they bring traditional Shanshui into the city, and endow large-scale urban buildings with a natural allure. Their recent projects, including Floating Island, Absolute Towers, Urban Forest in Chongqing, Shanshui City in Guiyang, the Shanshui complex in Nanjing, and the Chaoyang Park project in Beijing, have allowed them to gradually develop and refine the principles of Urban Shanshui. MAD's architectural practice does not avoid the problems of high-density cities and urbanization; rather, it attempts to inject the visionary realm of Shanshui into the modern city, dispelling the functionalist trends that have emerged since the Industrial Revolution, which see the city as a machine of population growth and material production. They seek a return to nature, guided by the spirit of Shanshui. Urban Shanshui design practice is the realization of the theory of the Shanshui City, emphasizing the viewpoint of "Shanshui in the world." This is most evident in the Guiyang Shanshui City and the Beijing Chaoyang Park proposals, both of which are large-scale architectural projects built within Central Business Districts in the city centers. Guiyang's Shanshui City remains a building on paper only, whereas the Beijing Chaoyang Park project is an earnest experiment in the development of a Shanshui City. The architects attempt to recreate the order of Shanshui within the city center, merging the culture of the natural world into a new form of contemporary city. The design is full of romanticism and imagination. It is a prophecy that points the way to the future of urban civilization.

The Shanshui City was initially proposed by Qian Xuesen. For a formal textual record, please see Qian Xuesen's July 31, 1990, letter to the scholar Wu Liangyong, "In recent years, I've been constantly thinking about one question: Can the aesthetics of China's pastoral poetry, classical gardens, and landscape paintings be combined to create a 'Shanshui city?' Even as they lived separate from the natural world, people would be returning to nature. Socialist China has the ability to build a Shanshui-style residential community." The concept of the Shanshui City arose from investigations into the construction of an ideal human habitat, and how to manage the relationship between humanity and nature. The capacity of the environment to support human life became the starting point for further development of the thinking behind the Shanshui City. Qian Xuesen's ideas are not limited to roads, buildings, and other principle features of the city; the thinking behind Shanshui planning, design, and construction takes into account people, animals, plants, climate, and other auxiliary conditions. This mode of thought stresses the importance of comprehensive urban planning.

The Shanshui city model is both ecological and humanistic. The goal of the urban Shanshui landscape is to unlock and make full use of the latent powers of nature and human creativity. At the same time, the Shanshui City model minimizes the ecological impact and environmental damage inherent to urban construction, achieving a result that is simultaneously beautiful, practical, and ecological. Shanshui construction stresses the organic integration of city and natural landscape. It is a new conception of urban civilization. Of course, while the idea of the Shanshui City has been raised before, it is lamentable that it has not been comprehensively realized within Chinese urban planning and architectural design practice. Fortunately, today there are young architects who have come to understand the academic and practical significance of the Shanshui City. Their designs operate as explorations of, and experiments in, the Shanshui City concept. MAD Architects were among the first to put the theory of the Shanshui City into practice. By positioning Shanshui City within the broader background of the history of contemporary architecture, they have integrated modern city life with the emotional experience of natural landscapes, transplanting Shanshui City from the realm of utopian ideals into contemporary urban reality.

Both the Shanshui City concept and MAD's architectural practice emphasize a dialogue between humans and nature. British scholar Joseph Needham expounded incisively on the relationship between ancient Chinese cities, architecture, and the natural world. He said, "There will never be another place that demonstrates so well how the Chinese passionately realize their grand principle that 'man cannot ever leave nature' [...] In the Imperial Palace, temples, and other great buildings, nature need not be mentioned. Whether in urban-rural concentrations or dispersed countryside homes, they all evoke a sense of universal pattern. And they all act as symbols, for the cardinal directions, the seasons, the winds, and the constellations." The principle that "man cannot ever leave nature" and the relationship between Chinese architecture and nature are both issues that we must explore today. The fruits of our research can perhaps offer an important academic foundation for the development of cities of the future. Architects aspire to developments that grow naturally out of their environments, in which the atmosphere of the natural world remains tangible. As Ma Yansong has realized, "[The Shanshui City]... would combine urban density and functionality with the aesthetic and philosophical ideals of Shanshui. It would be a city of the future built upon a core of spiritual and cultural values...." "When we speak of Shanshui Cities, our discussion is not limited to problems within Chinese cities, and we are not speaking of ink landscape painting [also called 'Shanshui' in Chinese]. Rather, we are discussing a particular emotional connection between man and nature, one which cannot be found in the West."

One could argue that Western master architects attach too much importance to modeling and space. The buildings they design approach a kind of perfection. Contemporary Chinese architects still do not come close to that level of perfection. Yet in Chinese art, there is something that cannot be expressed easily through language. It is not the clarity and perfection of Western architecture, but something ineffable which makes it possible to create an architecture that differs in significant ways from the Western tradition, to express a distinct architectural soul, a distinct metaphysical presence, and a distinct transcendent understanding. This architecture enables a dialogue with Shanshui to occur within the high-density urban environment—you could say it "combines a profound sense of humility in the face of nature with a lofty poetic sensibility to form an organic pattern that no other culture can surpass. In it, all buildings are integrated into the landscape" (Joseph Needham). It allows architecture to become an extension of nature, forming what Tang Dynasty poet Si Kong Tu called an "essence beyond flavor," an "image beyond the image, (a) landscape beyond the landscape," thus expanding the horizon of the imagination. It captures that elusive, exuberant quality that draws us into the abundant vital currents of a great city. This urban architecture is not just a translation of Western modern architecture, nor is it a "new edition" of traditional Chinese architecture, rather it defines a new landscape for architecture and for the city, exploring the essential meaning to be found within the future of urban civilization.

---

1. See Lin Zhongjie, *Kenzo Tange and the Metabolist Movement: Urban Utopias of Modern Japan*, Beijing: China Architecture & Building Press, 2011.

Wang Mingxian | Deputy Director, Institute of Architectural Art, Chinese National Academy of Arts

Wang Mingxian is a specialist in the fine arts, architectural aesthetics and contemporary architecture of post-1949 China. His publications include *Chinese Architectural Aesthetics Archive, A Pictorial History of Fine Arts in the New China: 1966–1976* (co-written with Yan Shanchun), and *The Possibility of Transcendence: Documenting 21st Century Chinese Architecture.*

MAD Architects

MAD Projects

Postscript

MAD Architects

Founded by Chinese architect Ma Yansong in 2004, MAD Architects is a global architecture firm committed to developing futuristic, organic, technologically advanced designs that embody a contemporary interpretation of the Eastern affinity for nature. With its core design philosophy of Shanshui City-a vision for the city of the future based in the spiritual and emotional needs of residents–MAD endeavors to create a balance between humanity, the city, and the environment.

Globally recognized as a creative pioneer, founding principal Ma is a central figure in the worldwide dialogue on the future of architecture. Ma was named one of the "10 Most Creative People in Architecture" by Fast Company in 2009. He received the prestigious "International Fellowship" from Royal Institute of British Architects (RIBA) in 2011, and was selected as "Young Global Leader (YGL)" by World Economic Forum (Davos Forum) in 2014.

In 2014, MAD was selected as principal designer for the Lucas Museum of Narrative Art (LMNA) in Chicago, USA, becoming the first China-based architecture firm to design an overseas cultural landmark. In 2006, MAD won the design competition for the Absolute Towers in Mississauga, Canada. The residential project is composed of 56-story and 50-story high-rises and was completed in 2012. The Council on Tall Buildings and Urban Habitat (CTBUH) awarded the towers "Best Tall Building Americas" in 2012 and EMPORIS ranked them first in their 2013 "Skyscraper Awards."

MAD has been commissioned by clients of various backgrounds to design mixed-use complexes, museums, theatres, social residences, renovations, artworks, and urban plans. Current ongoing urban projects include Chaoyang Park Plaza, a mixed-use complex project located in the new CBD of Beijing; Nanjing Zendai Himalayas Center, a city-scale urban development of approximate 600,000-square meter floor area; Huangshan Mountain Village, a master planning and architectural design project with 450,000-square meter site area. MAD's signature cultural projects include Harbin Cultural Island (under construction), Pingtan Art Museum (in design development stage), Ordos Museum (completed in 2011), and China Wood Sculpture Museum (completed in 2011).

MAD has ongoing international projects located in Rome, Paris, Japan, and Los Angeles. In the heart of Rome, MAD is designing a mixed-use courtyard building that reuses existing structure and will house apartments, office space, and a chapel with total usable area of approximately 28,000-square meter. In Paris, MAD was placed first in a competition with 96 contestant teams to build a residential complex on the right bank of the River Seine. In Japan, MAD delivered an organic design for a local education center. The firm's latest commission is a 13,000-square meter mixed-use residential complex in the center of Beverly Hills.

MAD has been a pioneer in contemporary art and design. MAD has participated in significant exhibitions in the 10th, 11th and 12th Venice Architecture Biennales. MAD also participated exhibitions at the Victoria and Albert Museum (London), the Louisiana Museum of Modern Art (Copenhagen), and MAXXI (Rome). An array of MAD's architecture models have been acquired by the well-known M+ Museum (Hong Kong) as part of their permanent collections.

The firm's design advances have been chronicled in a series of books: *Mad Dinner*, *Bright City*, *Ma Yansong*, and *Shanshui City*. MAD principals have been invited to speak at the American Institute of Architects, Architectural Association School of Architecture (London), World Economic Forum in Davos, Strelka Institute (Moscow), and the UCL Bartlett School of Architecture (London).

MAD Architects is currently led by Ma Yansong, Dang Qun and Yosuke Hayano and has offices in Beijing and Los Angeles.

MA YANSONG

Founding Principal

Beijing-born architect, Ma Yansong is recognized as an important voice in the new generation of architects. He is the first Chinese architect who has won an overseas landmark-building project. As the founder and principal of MAD Architects, Ma leads design across various scales. In recent years, many of Ma's designs follow his conception of the "Shanshui City," which is his vision to create a new balance among society, the city and the environment through new forms of architecture. Since designing the "Floating Island" in 2002, Ma has been putting this great idea into a world-wide practice through a series of imaginative works, including Absolute Towers, Hutong Bubble 32, Ordos Museum, China Wood Sculpture Museum, Fake Hills etc. Meanwhile, he has been exploring the cultural values of cities and architectures through domestic and international solo exhibitions, publications, and art works.

In 2006, Ma was awarded the "Young Architects Award" by the Architectural League of New York. In 2008 he was selected as one of the "20 Most Influential Young Architects" by ICON magazine. Fast Company respectively named him one of the "10 Most Creative People in Architecture in 2009" and one of the "100 Most Creative People in Business in 2014." In 2010 he became the first architect from China to receive a RIBA fellowship. In 2014 he was awarded "Young Global Leaders (YGL)" by World Economic Forum. In 2012, his iconic project Absolute Towers, two residential towers in Mississauga, Canada was named the "Best Tall Building in the Americas" by the Council on Tall Buildings and Urban Habitat (CTBUH).

Ma graduated from the Beijing Institute of Civil Engineering and Architecture, and holds a Master's Degree in Architecture from Yale University. He is currently a professor at Beijing University of Civil Engineering and Architecture.

DANG QUN

Principal

Born in Shanghai, Dang Qun is a partner at MAD Architects. She oversees project managements and corporate operations at MAD Architects, a global architect firm with over 80 staff members. She is also a key member in MAD strategy development.

Dang is a firm proponent of MAD's design philosophy "Shanshui City" and it's endeavors to pioneer technical innovations and green architecture for each project. Her outstanding abilities in cultivating a motivated team, driving operational efficiency, and her clear strategic direction enable projects to be realized with maximum respects to the design and ideology. Dang is closely involved in each process of MAD's series of projects, including Absolute Towers, Ordos Museum, China Wood Sculpture Museum, Fake Hills, Chaoyang Park Plaza, Nanjing Zendai Himalayas Center, Harbin Cultural Island, and the Lucas Museum of Narrative Art, etc.

Dang holds a Master's Degree in Architecture from Iowa State University and received a Certificate of Merit from the American Institute of Architects in 2000. Dang's academic career includes a visiting professorship at Pratt Institute, and assistant professor ship at Iowa State University.

YOSUKE HAYANO

Principal

Born in Aichi, Japan, Yosuke Hayano is a first-class registered architect in Japan. He is responsible for all design work from concept stage to construction stage including all technical aspects as well as managing all design teams in the office. He was the winner of 2006 Architecture League of New York Young Architects Award, 2011 Design for Asia award, and 2011 Kumamoto Artpolis Award.

Yosuke Hayano received his Bachelor of Materials Engineering from Waseda University in Tokyo in 2000, Associate degree in Architecture at Waseda Art and Architecture School in 2001, and his post Master's in Architecture at the Architectural Association of London in 2003. He was a visiting lecturer at Waseda Art and Architecture School from 2008 until 2012 and at Tokyo University from 2010 until 2012.

MAD Projects

Nanjing Zendai Himalayas Center

2012–2017 | Nanjing, China
Type : Urban Complex—Commercial, Office, Residential, Hotel
Status: Under Construction
Site area : 93,595 sqm
Building area : 567,844 sqm
Building height : 120 m

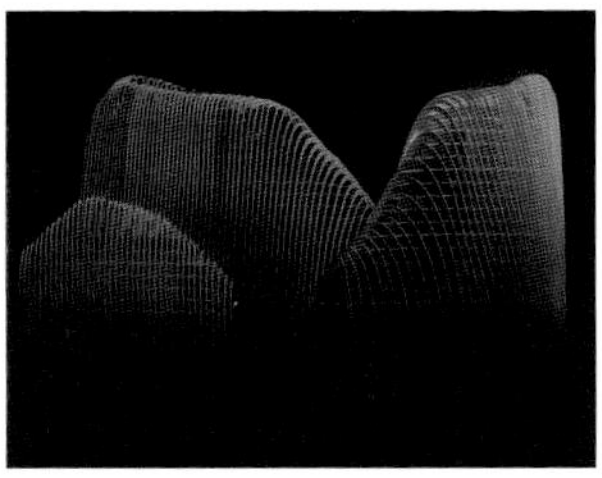

Chaoyang Park Plaza

2012–2016 | Pingtan, China
Type : Urban complex—Office, Commercial, Residential
Status : Under Construction
Site area : 30,763 sqm
Building area: 223,000 sqm
Building height : 120 m

Pingtan Art Museum

2011–2017 | Pingtan, China
Type: Museum
Site area : 32,000 sqm
Building area : 40,000 sqm

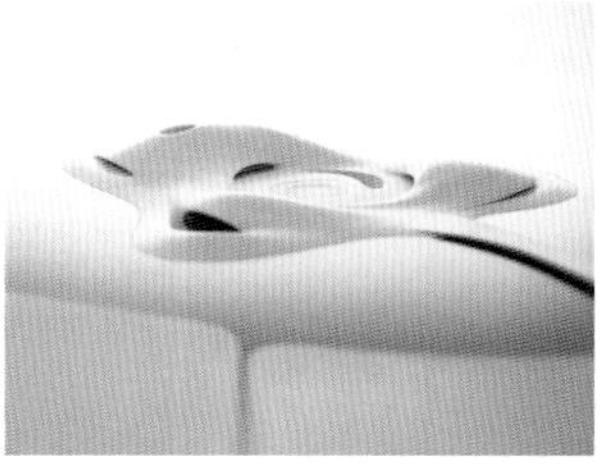

Ordos Museum

2005–2011 | Ordos, China
Type : Museum
Site area : 27,760 sqm
Building area : 41,227 sqm
Building height: 40 m

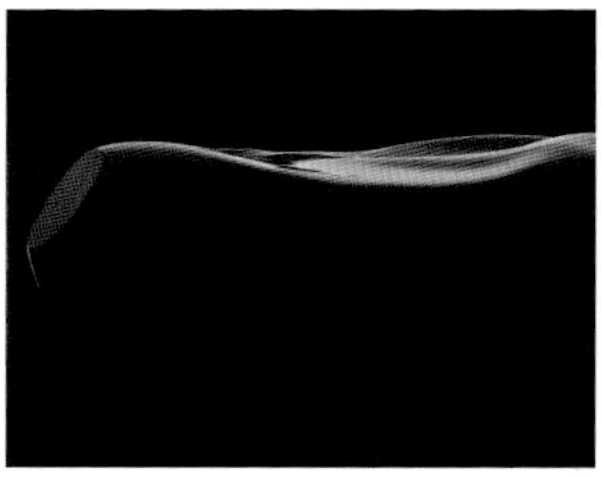

China Wood Sculpture Museum

2009–2013 | Harbin, China
Type: Museum
Building area: 12,959 sqm
Building height: 21 m

Absolute Towers

2006–2012 | Mississauga, Canada
Type : Apartment
Tower A : 45,000 sqm, 56 stories / height 170 m
Tower B : 40,000 sqm, 50 stories / height 150 m

Fake Hills

2010–2016 | Beihai, China
Type : Residential
Status : Under construction
Site area : 109,203 sqm
Building area : 492,369 sqm
Building height : Slab 106 m, Tower 194 m

Harbin Culture Center

2010–2014 | Harbin, China
Type : Theater, Cultural Center
Site area : 1,700,000 sqm
Building area : 72,275 sqm

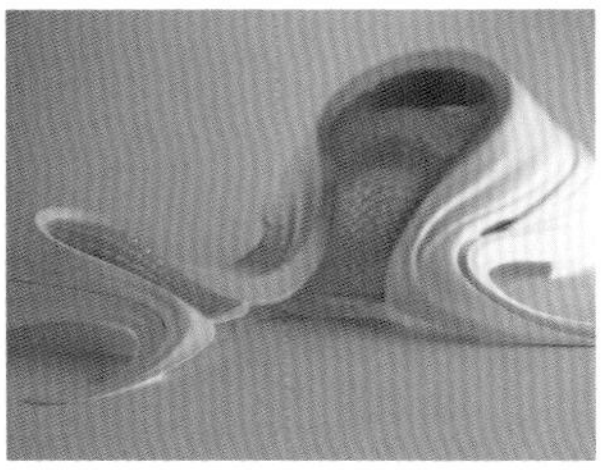

Huangshan Mountain Village

2009–2015 | Huangshan, China
Type : Apartment, Commercial, Community Complex
Status : Under construction
Site area : 102,900 sqm
Building area : 70,000 sqm
Building height : 60 m

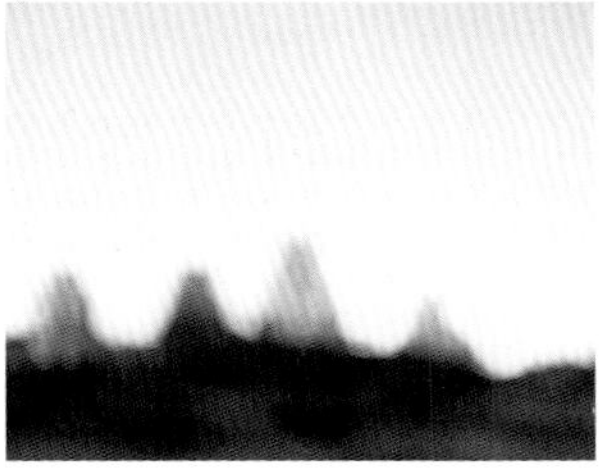

Fish Tank

2004
Size : 300(L) × 300(W) × 400(H) mm

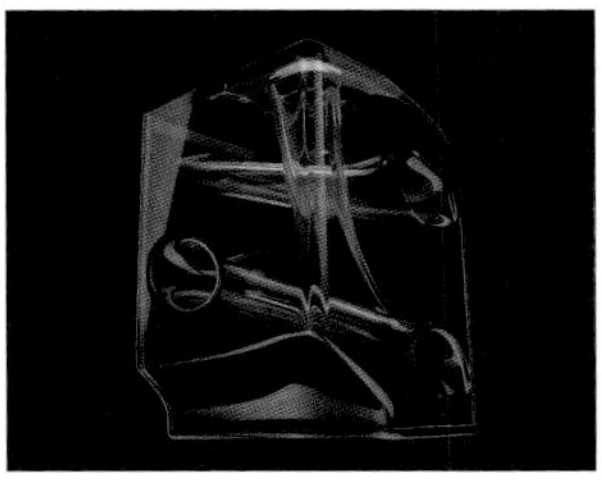

Afterword

The publication of this book coincides with MAD Architects' tenth anniversary. I would like to thank our advisor Bao Pao for his deep interest in our work over the years, and for the ways he has both challenged and inspired our thinking. Thanks are also due to my partner, Dang Qun, for her unwavering faith and courage in confronting all manner of difficulties, and for the hard work she put into making Shanshui City a reality.

Kenya Hara is not only the designer of this book, but also a valued teacher and friend. I thank him for facilitating the creation of this book. I would also like thank critics Hans-Ulrich Obrist, Lorenza Baroncelli, Wang Mingxian, and Li Xiangning for their contributions.

Finally I wish to thank Chen Shuyu, Ye Cheng, and Qu Hui for their strenuous editorial and organizational efforts.

Ma Yansong
September 1, 2014

SHANSHUI CITY

MA YANSONG

Concept	Ma Yansong
Art Direction	Kenya Hara
Design	Kenya Hara + Kaoru Matsuno
Photography: Models	Takashi Sekiguchi,
Photography: Architecture	Iwan Baan, Xia Zhi, Tom Arban, Chi Peng, Cai Guoqiang
Coordination MAD	Chen Shuyu, Ye Cheng, Qu Hui
Coordination LMP	Anna Schiestl
Translation (Chi-Eng)	Joshua Dyer, Patrick Rhine
Proofreading	Anna Roos
Printing and binding	Artron Art (Group) Co., Ltd.
Paper	157gsm MERTHA Bright art paper

Lars Müller Publishers
Zürich, Switzerland
www.lars-mueller-publishers.com

ISBN 978-3-03778-457-0

Printed in China